READING LAO TZU

READING LAO TZU

A Companion to the *Tao Te Ching*

with a New Translation

Ha Poong Kim

To order additional copies of this book, contact:
Xlibris Corporation
1-888-795-4274
www.Xlibris.com
Orders@Xlibris.com
17038

To Dorothee

CONTENTS

PREFACE

This book is intended for those who seek direct access to Lao Tzu's meaning in the *Tao Te Ching*. First time readers of this classic generally find it all but impossible to comprehend its key passages, which more often than not contain cryptic lines and paradoxical logic. I have written my commentary primarily to aid such readers. For this reason, my comments eschew scholarly discussions, focusing on Lao Tzu's meaning in particular passages.

It was nearly twenty years ago when I made my first attempt to translate the *Tao Te Ching*, partly to force myself to study the text closely, and partly to provide my own translation for the course I was then teaching in Chinese philosophy. What I produced was a translation of about fifty of the eighty-one chapters, since I avoided those passages that I found too abstruse or simply unintelligible. During the following years until my retirement, I returned to the text now and again, translating more chapters, while also reworking the earlier versions. Then, a few years ago, I decided to write this commentary especially for those new to Lao Tzu.

According to one author, there are supposed to be "several hundred extant commentaries" on the *Lao Tzu*.[1] I am adding one more. In some instances I follow the traditional reading of the text; in others, I do not. What one must keep in mind is that agreement or disagreement in this case is simply a matter of interpretation. And there is no "true" or "false" interpretation in the sense of grasping or missing some "absolute" or "objective" meaning of the text. I ask that my reader take my comments as he or she would an art critic's remarks on art objects.

By Lao Tzu's "meaning" in a given passage, I do not mean *the* meaning of the passage in some "absolute" or "objective" sense, but its meaning as I take it to be. I am well aware of the debate among philosophers and literary theorists concerning the text and its meaning. This is obviously no place to take up such an academic exercise. Let me simply state that I speak of "the meaning" of a particular passage in a way analogous to the way we speak of "the shape" of a physical object in everyday speech. Suppose you say: "The shape of this house is octagonal." By so saying, you wouldn't necessarily be reporting on "the shape" of the house in some absolute sense, independent of any viewpoint. Clearly, the shape of the house varies depending on the viewpoint from which it is seen. There isn't "the shape" of the house seen from no particular perspective. In other words, "the shape" of the house is necessarily relative to the viewer's angle of vision. Analogously, "the meaning" of the text is inevitably relative to the reader's perspective.

I am happy to acknowledge that two of my children contributed significantly to the genesis of this work. Alan read the earlier version, which was almost twice as long as this one, and provided extensive criticisms, both editorial and philosophical. It was upon his urging that I decided to write the present, shorter version. Natalie read my final draft with her usual thoroughness, and made numerous editorial suggestions. My thanks go to Sandra Mattielli and Carol and Joseph Christen for their help with the cover art.

I dedicate this book to my wife, Dorothee. Without her loving support and encouragement, I would not have completed it.

Notes

1 See Chan (1979), p. ix.

INTRODUCTION

Who was Lao Tzu? Did a historical person by that name actually exist? If he did, did he actually write the *Tao Te Ching*? The oldest historical information concerning Lao Tzu is given in Ssu-ma Ch'ien's *Shih Chi*, written in the first century B.C. According to this record, Lao Tzu's family name was Li, his personal name Erh and his *tzu*[1] Tan. Ssu-ma Ch'ien writes that Lao Tzu authored the *Tao Te Ching* in two books and was a contemporary of Confucius (551-479 B.C.). This date is questionable, however, because, according to the brief genealogy of his descendants given in the same biography, Lao Tzu would have to be a younger contemporary of Mencius (372?-289? B.C.)—that is, nearly two centuries after Confucius. It seems that Lao Tzu was a half-legendary figure even in antiquity. Ssu-ma Chi'en writes: "Lao Tzu is said to have lived over 160 years. Some say he lived 200 years."

Aside from the uncertainty surrounding the authorship of the *Tao Te Ching*, scholars also debate the dating of the work itself. The prevailing view today is that the bulk of the text was written during the first half of the fourth century B.C.—that is, during the early part of the Warring States period, the time of great upheavals preceding the first unification of China. I subscribe to this view.[2] This dating would place the appearance of the work roughly a century after the death of Confucius and make it almost contemporaneous with the appearance of the *Mencius* and the *Chuang Tzu*.[3]

There are different versions of the *Tao Te Ching*. Their variations are, however, largely insignificant as they vary mostly in individual words or composition. The standard version today is that used in the commentary by Wang Pi (226-249). I have used for my work the Meiwa (Ming-ho) edition,[4] a Wang Pi version. In the past few decades, three ancient texts have been discovered: the "Ma-wang-tui Texts"[5] (in 1973) and the "Bamboo Slip Lao Tzu"[6] (in 1993). These texts—especially the latter—do show some variations from the Wang Pi text. However, they interest us little, since we are primarily concerned with the reading of the *Tao Te Ching* as we find it in its standard version.

In my translation, I have tried to be as faithful as possible to the text, often at the cost of intelligibility or palatability. I believe this approach is justified, especially in view of the fact that resistance to easy accessibility characterizes the *Tao Te Ching* and is, indeed, one of the reasons why this work, more than any other classics of Chinese antiquity, calls for help from commentaries. Any attempt to make intelligible in the translation what is not so in the original inevitably introduces the translator's interpretation in the process. Needless to say, interpretation properly belongs to commentary, not to the text.

The Chinese text of the *Tao Te Ching* has numerous rhymed passages, but it is by no means in verse throughout.[7] In my translation, however, I have adopted verse form for the entire work, in order to give some sense of the music of the original, unmistakable even in passages not in rhyme.[8]

One special note on what may seem to be Lao Tzu's puzzling use of the word "therefore"[9] in many passages. This connective often occurs where there seems no apparent connection at all between what comes before it and what comes after it. This may cause some disruption in reading. But one need not *look for* any logical connection between what precedes the connective and what follows it.[10] As a matter of fact, it is often the case that no such connection is intended in the text. However, one may sometimes recognize a connection where one initially did not by conventional thinking, as one begins to appreciate Lao Tzu's own logic and style.[11]

In my commentary, I avoid line-by-line exegesis, thus omitting discussion of many passages. Such passages include not only those lines whose meaning is obvious or straightforward, but also those whose meaning may not be so obvious, yet may be graspable in light of my earlier comments.[12] In the *Tao Te Ching*, one frequently comes across the same or similar lines appearing again and again. Also, in some instances, the same idea is expressed repeatedly in different images or formulations, often only with slight variations. This is particularly the case with passages expressing the main themes of the work. I do not comment on such passages in order not to repeat the same point over and over again, but at the same time as a way of inviting the reader's active, rather than passive, reading.

The *Tao Te Ching* has no particular thematic order or development, so that it may be read at random. However, I must say, my commentary may best be read in the order in which the chapters appear, as later comments presuppose earlier ones.

Finally, a few words on the Appendices. There is no question that the central teachings of the *Tao Te Ching* are the very antithesis of those of Confucius. Indeed, many key passages are clearly aimed against certain Confucian ideas. In my commentary, however, I avoid discussing Lao Tzu's attack on Confucius's teachings. Appendix I is devoted to this subject. Appendix II is a short meditation on the Taoist sage as the "enlightened" one. The term "sage" occurs in the *Tao Te Ching* numerous times, almost as frequently as the term "Tao." In most instances, Lao Tzu speaks of the sage as the ideal ruler. However, there are several passages that suggest the sage as a man who has attained the "enlightened" state of awareness. In this Appendix, I explore Lao Tzu's vision of the sage especially in view of these passages.

Notes

[1]   A *tzu* is a second name that a man adopts, in addition to his given name. An adult man is commonly addressed by his *tzu*, rather than by his given name.

[2]   I take this view primarily in view of the central teachings of the work. It has recently received a strong confirmation from a study based on a careful analysis of the language and genre of the text. See William H. Baxter, "Situating

the Language of the *Lao-tzu*: The Probable Date of the *Tao-te-ching*" included in Livia Kohn and Michael LaFargue (eds.), *Lao-tzu and the Tao-te-ching*.

3 These are two important works of the same period. This period was perhaps the most fertile time in the intellectual history of China, which saw the flourishing of "One Hundred Schools."

4 A Japanese edition, originally published in 1770. I have used the edition contained in Fukunaga Mitsuji, *Rōshi* (Lao Tzu), 2 Vols.

5 Discovered in the tomb of a Han nobleman buried in 168 B.C. The two texts are included in Robert G. Henricks (tr.), *Lao Tzu: Te-Tao Ching*.

6 Discovered in a tomb in Guodian (Kuo-tien), Hubei province. It is so called because it was written on strips of bamboo, which have survived since 300 B.C. The text, also known as "Guodian Laozi," contains less than a half of the passages in the standard edition. See Robert G. Henricks (tr.), *Lao Tzu's Tao Te Ching*.

7 For a pioneering study of the poetry of the *Tao Te Ching*, see Bernhard Karlgren, "The Poetical Parts in Lao-Tsi," *Göteborgs Högskolas Årsskrift*, XXXVIII (1932:3).

8 I have versified the text in light of Fukunaga Mitsuji's punctuation throughout. Fukunaga's reading of rhymed passages follows Chu Ch'ien-chih's *Lao-tzu chiao-shih* (Shanghai, 1958).

9 In most instances, "therefore" is my translation of the character *ku*. But sometimes *shih i* is also translated as "therefore."

10 This approach is perhaps justified in view of the fact that the character *ku* is sometimes used merely as a rhetorical device for transition in a passage, rather than as a connective signifying a causal or logical connection. Waley notes that this word often has a meaning "transitional between 'Truly' [sic] and 'therefore'." (See Waley, p. 247.) He translates it "truly" as well as "therefore" in his translation of the *Tao Te Ching*.

11 It may be pointed out that the sort of difficulty that I am speaking of here is precisely the same sort of difficulty that the reader of the Chinese text also faces—that is, regarding many instances of *ku* and *shih i*. I have decided to reproduce this difficulty in this translation, instead of trying to eliminate it. In my view, it is the sort of hurdle that the reader of this difficult work must himself or herself overcome to grasp its central teachings.

12 The *Tao Te Ching* contains many passages whose meaning is uncertain for

various possible reasons such as textual corruption or lacunae. Generally, I forgo commenting on such passages.

TRANSLATION

AND

COMMENTARY

BOOK ONE

TAO

CHAPTER 1

1 *No Tao that may be Tao is the constant Tao;*
2 *No name that may be a name is the constant name.*
3 *By non-being you name the beginning of Heaven and Earth;*
4 *By being you name the mother of the ten thousand things.*
5 *Therefore, always free of desire you see the secret;*
6 *Always with desire you see its appearance.*
7 *These two*
8 *Are the same in origin yet different in name.*
9 *Their sameness may be called a mystery.*
10 *It is the mystery beyond mysteries,*
11 *The gate to myriad secrets.*

Lao Tzu's ultimate topic is Tao, the true way. The basic meaning of the character *tao* is "way" or "road." However, it has also a figurative meaning of "method," "principle," "true way" or "right way." In the opening lines, Lao Tzu confronts the reader with riddle-like announcements. His intention is to prepare the reader for his teaching of the unspeakable, hence unteachable, Tao. How can one teach what is unteachable? Only by going beyond the bounds of the word. Hence his paradoxical style.

Why is Tao unspeakable? This has to do with the infinite nature of Tao as much as with the limiting nature of language. For Lao Tzu Tao is that which eternally *is*, beyond the phenomenal world. That is why he calls it the "constant Tao." What is "constant" is not time-bound, unlike all finite things, which come and go. Tao is beyond the reach of the senses, so he calls it the "Invisible," the "Inaudible," and the "Intangible."[1] Tao is what phenomenal existence is not. It is "infinite" in the sense of not having the finite (or definite) nature of phenomenal objects. But words necessarily limit what they refer to. Therefore Tao is unspeakable.

By "Tao that may be Tao" Lao Tzu means Tao taught or spoken of. But Tao spoken of cannot be the "constant Tao," for no word can express what is infinite. In the second line, Lao Tzu asserts the same thesis by pointing out the impossibility of the "constant name." The "constant name" means the "name of the constant Tao," which is an oxymoron, since a name necessarily qualifies or limits what it designates. Thus Tao is nameless.

Lines 3-4[2] may best be read in light of the ancient Chinese cosmology, which regarded Heaven and Earth (*t'ien ti*) as the ultimate source of all beings.[3] To a certain extent, Lao Tzu accepts this view, but he goes beyond it, by asserting that Heaven and Earth, in turn, arise from Tao. In these lines, Lao Tzu expresses this universal lineage of life in terms of "being" (*yu*) and "non-being" (*wu*).[4] "The beginning of Heaven and Earth"[5] refers to that from which Heaven and Earth arise, namely, Tao, while "the mother of the ten thousand things" refers to that from which all things come into being, namely, Heaven and Earth. By calling the former "non-being" and the latter "being," he is declaring the rise of what *is* (or what is named or nameable) from what *is not* (or what is nameless). It is remarkable that Lao Tzu is here assigning Heaven and Earth, too, to the domain of the finite, along with the ten thousand things.[6]

How does one recognize the infinite Tao? Lao Tzu says: "Therefore, always free of desire you see the secret." It is the desiring mind that discriminates and sees the ten thousand things. With that mind gone, the phenomenal world of the many disappears, and there appears the "undifferentiated" One.[7] On the other hand, Lao Tzu goes on to say: "Always with desire you see its appearance." For him the visible world *is* Tao in "appearance"; it is not something altogether groundless or illusory.

Thus, in the next two lines, Lao Tzu announces the identity ("sameness") of the nameless Tao and the named world. The nameless is nowhere outside the named, as the invisible is nowhere outside the visible. This identity of the two will remain a "mystery," however, as long as the "nameless" remains a mere name. Only when you go beyond the domain of names (opposites) will their identity cease to be a "mystery."

Notes

[1]   Ch. 14.

[2]   In my translation, I depart from the common rendering of these two lines. According to this reading, the passage may be translated as "Nameless is the beginning of Heaven and Earth;/ Named is the mother of the ten thousand things." See, e.g., Chan (1963a), p. 139; Lau, p. 57.

[3]   Heaven as the supreme ruler of the universe, and Earth as the nurturer of all living things.

[4]   This lineage is more directly stated in Ch. 40.

[5]   A similar phrase, "the root of Heaven and Earth," appears in Ch. 6.

[6]   In Ch. 39 Lao Tzu expresses the finiteness of Heaven and Earth, along with that of "spirits," "valleys," and the "ten thousand things."

[7]   See Ch. 25, where one reads: "There is something undifferentiated/ That precedes the birth of Heaven and Earth."

CHAPTER 2

1   *All under Heaven recognize beautiful as beautiful,*
2   *But this is none other than ugly.*
3   *Everyone recognizes good as good,*
4   *But this is none other than bad.*
5   *Therefore being and non-being rise together;*
6   *Difficult and easy complete each other;*
7   *Long and short shape each other;*
8   *High and low lean on each other;*
9   *Sound and voice come in harmony;*
10 *Front and back accompany each other.*
11 *Therefore the sage*
12 *Relies on no-action,*
13 *Practices wordless teaching.*
14 *There rise the ten thousand things, but he disowns nothing,*
15 *He gives them life, yet does not possess them;*
16 *Rules them, yet does not depend on them;*
17 *His work is done, but he never dwells in it.*
18 *Truly, since he never dwells,*
19 *He never departs.*

This chapter has two parts. In the first part (lines 1-10), Lao Tzu points out the correlative nature of all opposites, which exist only in the domain of names, not in the nameless. People, however, take as absolute what is merely relative. "All under Heaven recognize beautiful as beautiful"—as if beauty were in the thing they find "beautiful." But "beautiful" is a name, which means nothing except as the correlative of its opposite, "ugly." By asserting the equality of "beautiful" and "ugly," Lao Tzu rejects the opposition between the two and, thereby, both concepts, at the same time. From the nameless standpoint of Tao, there is neither "beautiful" nor "ugly." Similarly, there is neither "good" nor "bad." Lines 3-4 may be read as Lao Tzu's denial of the ethical distinction of "good" and "bad." In the next six lines we read a list of co-rising opposites, such as "being"/"non-being,"[1] "difficult"/"easy," and "long"/"short." What is true of "beautiful" and "ugly" is, of course, also true of these correlatives.

As we turn to the second part, let me say a few words about the Chinese concept of *sheng jen*, the term translated here and later as "sage." *Sheng jen* literally means "holy man." Its standard translation as "sage" is acceptable insofar as a *sheng jen* is a man of profound wisdom. However, it must be kept in mind, he is more than just a wise man; he is a man whose qualities are such that his proper place in the human world is to rule and bring a universal peace to all under Heaven. It is for this reason that sagehood and ideal rulership are inseparable.[2]

In lines 11-12, Lao Tzu presents the sage as a man of "no-action" (*wu-wei*). By "no-action" he means an act of immediacy, devoid of human intentionality. It is the denial of thought-mediated act. Such is nature's doing, immediate and spontaneous. The sage lives in the domain of the nameless. Therefore his action is "no-action," which is his "wordless teaching."

In the remaining lines, Lao Tzu describes the sage's rule through "no-action." The sage rules his people, as Heaven and Earth rule the ten thousand things: he disowns no one, possesses nothing, depends on no one, and dwells in nothing.

Notes

[1]   In line 5, Lao Tzu states the co-rising of "being" and "non-being." The reader may ask how this statement can be reconciled with what we earlier took to be his meaning in the following lines of Ch. 1: "By non-being you name the beginning of Heaven and Earth;/ By being you name the mother of the ten thousand things." What is important to keep in mind is that in these lines Lao Tzu is using the *concepts* of "being" and "non-being" (which

are indeed correlatives), in stating the universal lineage of life. He is not asserting that Tao is some *absolute* "non-being," out of which all "beings" arise. See my comment on Ch. 40.

2   The three legendary kings of Chinese antiquity, Yao, Shun and Yü, are traditionally called *sheng wang*, meaning "sage kings." Understandably, different schools have different conceptions of "sage," as *sheng jen* represents for each its ideal ruler as well as its ideal man.

CHAPTER 3

1   *If you do not exalt the worthy,*
2   *You will keep the people from contention.*
3   *If you do not treasure rare goods,*
4   *You will keep them from stealing.*
5   *If you do not exhibit things that may arouse their desire,*
6   *You will keep their minds in peace.*
7   *Therefore the sage, in governing the people,*
8   *Makes their minds empty,*
9   *Their stomachs full,*
10 *Their ambitions weak,*
11 *Their bones strong.*
12 *He always makes the people unknowing and undesiring,*
13 *Keeps the clever ones from daring to act.*
14 *He acts through no-action, and everything is in order.*

Why do people contend? In pursuit of names. Why do people steal? To own rare goods. Why are people unhappy? Because of their greed. But what are names, rare goods and greed? They are all products of human civilization. Abandon name-mediated, abstract values, and return to life in nature, to the nameless.

Evident in lines 7-12 is the primacy of biological existence—the sort of existence that we humans share with our unknowing, unspeaking fellow creatures. It is life in its strictest sense, as every living being immediately identifies with it. I say "immediately" because it is life unmediated—that is, prior to mediation of "death." It is life in nature.

Humanity has separated itself from nature, thanks to its name-mediated knowledge and desires. This alienated state is precisely what civilization is. The sage teaches the return of humanity to nameless life in nature. That is why he "always makes the people unknowing [*wu chih*] and undesiring [*wu yü*]." Note here that "unknowing" means freedom from name-mediated knowledge; it does not mean the denial of "knowing" at the immediate, biological level. (Doesn't every creature immediately "know" what it needs for its survival?) Similarly, "undesiring" does not mean the utter absence of desires; it means freedom from the name-mediated desires of civilization.

CHAPTER 4

1   *Tao is empty,*
2   *You may use it but never fill it.*
3   *Fathomless, it is like the progenitor of the ten thousand things.*
4   *[It] blunts the sharpness,*
5   *Unravels the tangles,*
6   *Softens the brilliance,*
7   *Identifies with the dust.*
8   *Deep and still, it seems as though existing forever.*
9   *I don't know whose son it is.*
10 *It bears the image of God's forefather.*

Tao is "empty" in that it is devoid of all finite qualities. Not that it is nothing, to be sure. Tao is the inexhaustible spring of the ten thousand things. It is infinite: "fathomless" and "deep and still."

Tao is "constant": there never was time when it was not. So Lao Tzu declares: "I don't know whose son it is." It looks more like "God's forefather."

(For lines 4-7,[1] see my comment on Chapter 56, where they appear again.)

Notes

[1] These four lines interrupt the unity and flow of the chapter. Takeuchi Yoshio regards their occurrence as an error. He notes the rhyming of the remaining lines without the intrusion of lines 4-7. See Takeuchi, p. 183.

Chapter 5

1 *Heaven and Earth are not humane:*
2 *They treat the ten thousand things as straw dogs.*
3 *The sage is not humane:*
4 *He treats the people as straw dogs.*
5 *The space between Heaven and Earth—*
6 *Is it not as though it were a bellows?*
7 *It is empty, yet inexhaustible.*
8 *Ever active, it gives off more and more.*
9 *Much talk inevitably leads to predicament.*
10 *It is better to hold on to the void.*[1]

Why is the sage "not humane"? Why does he "treat his people as straw dogs"?[2] Because he has gone beyond the morality of "humane" (*jen*) and "not humane" (*pu jen*). His is the nameless perspective of Tao. He is inhumane only in the language of *jen* and *pu jen*. The same may be said of Heaven and Earth, and indeed of Tao. But this would only reflect humanity's anthropocentric view of the universe.

Does Lao Tzu lament the inhumanity of Tao? Of course not. One may call his view of the universe naturalistic. Notice his naturalistic tone in lines 5-8, where he speaks of the "space between Heaven and Earth" as a sort of cosmic "bellows," which is "empty" yet "ever active."

The more you talk, the farther you go away from the truth. For Tao is unspeakable. "It is better to hold on to the void." To the nameless.

Notes

1   Read *chung* as a variant of *ch'ung*. See Fukunaga, Vol. 1, p. 72.
2   In ancient China "straw dogs" (*ch'u kou*) were used for purposes of exorcism at sacrificial rites; once the rite was over, they were simply thrown away.

CHAPTER 6

1   *The spirit of the mountain gorge never dies.*
2   *It is called the mysterious female.*
3   *The gate of the mysterious female—*
4   *It is called the root of Heaven and Earth.*
5   *Never ceasing to be, it seems as though existing forever.*
6   *Use never exhausts it.*

Lao Tzu identifies the "spirit of the mountain gorge" as the "mysterious female" on account of its fertility. This "spirit" is none other than the ever-productive Tao: the eternal source of life. From the mountain gorge flows the stream that gives life to the ten thousand things. Tao is "the root of Heaven and Earth." Lao Tzu calls it "the gate of the mysterious female." Notice his use of the elemental images of "gate" and "root," both of which suggest the physiology of the female reproductive organs.[1]

Notes

[1]   In his commentary on this chapter, Wang Pi writes: "'The spirit of the mountain gorge' is the non-being (*wu*) in the center of the gorge." Katō Jōken identifies the "gate of the mysterious female" as "the female genitalia that gave birth to Heaven and Earth. See Katō, pp. 20, 30.

CHAPTER 7

1   *Heaven and Earth are everlasting.*
2   *The reason why they are everlasting*
3   *Is that they do not live for themselves.*
4   *That is why they can live long.*
5   *Therefore the sage*
6   *Puts himself last and finds himself first;*
7   *He leaves himself out and finds himself preserved.*
8   *Is it not because he is selfless*
9   *That he can fulfill himself?*

Heaven and Earth are "selfless" (*wu szu*), and so is the sage. The character *szu* means "private self," which implies separateness from the whole, the loss of oneness with Tao. Lao Tzu finds humans alone pursue their own way, separate from the whole; they have lost their oneness with Tao.

But the sage is one with Tao. That is why he is long-lasting. Whoever pursues his private way fails. Do you seek to "fulfill yourself"? Be selfless and follow Tao.

CHAPTER 8

1   *The supreme good is like water.*
2   *Water benefits the ten thousand things, yet contends with*
     nothing.
3   *It dwells where everyone is loath to be.*
4   *That is why it is near to Tao.*
5   *In dwelling, the good is the ground,*
6   *In thought, the good is depth,*
7   *In association, the good is gentleness,*
8   *In speech, the good is truthfulness,*
9   *In government, the good is order,*
10   *In work, the good is ability.*
11   *In movement, the good is timeliness.*
12   *Truly, because it [water] contends with nothing,*
13   *It is beyond reproach.*

Water nourishes all living things, yet it "contends with nothing," because it is selfless. Being selfless, "it dwells where everyone is loath to be."

In lines 5-11 one reads a list of "goods" (*shan*). But these lines interrupt the unity and flow of the chapter.[1] I take them to be a later interpolation, which has little to do with Lao Tzu's own teachings.

Notes

[1] I agree with Takeuchi Yoshio, who suggests that the chapter should be read without these lines. He points out that they are out of place thematically. He also notes Wang Pi's silence on them in his commentary. See Takeuchi, p. 191. See also Lau, p. 64n.

CHAPTER 9

1   *Rather than hold the bowl until it fills to the brim,*
2   *Better quit in time.*
3   *Hammer the blade to its sharpest,*
4   *And you will be unable to preserve it long.*
5   *Fill the hall with gold and jade,*
6   *And you will be unable to keep them safe.*
7   *He who is arrogant with his wealth and position*
8   *Will bring calamity upon himself.*
9   *To withdraw when the task is accomplished*
10   *Is the way of Heaven.*

Why would one "hold the bowl until it fills to the brim"? Why would a sword-smith "hammer the sword to its sharpest"? Why would anyone try to "fill the hall with gold and jade"? All because of man's desire for more and more. We call this "greed," which one finds only among humans. Greed derives from man's name-mediated desires. There is no greed in the nameless universe of animals; they live in immediacy, each following its Tao-appointed nature.

Every living thing has some desire or other that is necessary for its existence and natural to its being. Such are all biological desires. They rise and recede, depending on the creature's needs. Man's name-mediated desires are different, although their origin too may be traced to some particular natural desires. They are abstract values, which we humans acquire as we learn to speak. Once acquired, they gain hold of our minds, independently of our needs—often to the detriment of our very well-being. We pursue our man-made desires, never knowing when to stop.

CHAPTER 10

1   *Rest your shining spirit and embrace the One.*
2   *Can you forever hold onto it?*
3   *Concentrate your breath and attain the utmost softness.*
4   *Can you become a baby?*
5   *Clean your mysterious mirror.*
6   *Can you keep it free of blemish?*
7   *Love the people and keep the state in peace.*
8   *Can you rule through no-action?*
9   *As the gate of Heaven opens and closes,*
10 *Can you play the female part?*
11 *As bright light reaches all four directions,*
12 *Can you remain unknowing?*
13 *To give people life and nurture them;*
14 *To give them life, without possessing them;*
15 *To rule them, without depending on them;*
16 *To lead them, without directing them—*
17 *This is called the mysterious Te.*

Of all creatures, only we humans have left the nameless state of nature, pursuing our own way, namely, civilization. How are we then to return to our original state, freeing ourselves from the universe of names and values? That is the most fundamental existential question that each human being faces. I read this chapter in light of this ultimate question.

The "shining spirit" refers to the lively spirit. Thus, the opening line may be read to mean: Bring to rest your active spirit, "embracing the One [*pao i*]," namely, Tao.[1]

Lines 3-4. "Concentrate your breath [*ch'i*],"[2] so that you may attain the baby-like softness. Note that Lao Tzu says later in Chapter 76:

"Therefore the hard and strong are companions of death,/ The soft and weak are companions of life."

Lines 5-6. Can you keep your transcendental "mirror" unobstructed by the visible?

How does one "love the people and keep the state in peace"? By ruling according to Tao, that is, by not ruling.

Lines 9-10 have been variously interpreted.[3] I read them to mean: As you live through your phenomenal existence,[4] can you "play the female part"—that is, live the life of non-contention and passivity, rather than that of contention and activity?

Lines 11-12. Can you remain free of all name-mediated thoughts, as the present reveals itself in the "bright light" of Tao?[5]

The character *te* is commonly translated as "virtue" in English.[6] But Lao Tzu uses it in a non-ethical sense of "power" or "potency." By the "mysterious Te" he is referring to Tao's life-giving, life-nurturing power. Tao's power is "mysterious" in that it is invisible. Lao Tzu recognizes the same "mysterious Te" in the sage's power to benefit his people as well as in the power of Heaven and Earth to give life to the ten thousand things. The sage's Te is Tao's, not his personal power. Indeed, he exercises this "mysterious Te," because he is selfless—just like Heaven and Earth.

Notes

[1]   This phrase "embrace the One" (*pao i*) reappears later in Ch. 22. It also appears twice (once its variant) in the *Chuang Tzu*. See *Chuang Tzu*, Chs. 11 and 23; Watson, pp. 119-120, 253. It seems that the phrase was a common expression used by the Taoists of antiquity.

[2]   Commentators generally agree that this line refers to some sort of breathing exercise. Waley calls it "Taoist yoga." See his discussion on the subject in Appendix III, Waley, pp. 116-120.

[3]   See, e.g., Waley, p. 154 and Chan (1963b), p. 118.

[4]   I take line 9 to refer to the ongoing process of phenomenal existence.

[5]   See Appendix II.

[6]   This is justifiable, insofar as the character is used in the ethical sense of "moral virtue," as is generally the case in Confucian literature. But the term is too rich

to be considered the Chinese equivalent of the English word "virtue" used today. It is closer to the Latin word *virtus*.

CHAPTER 11

1   *Thirty spokes share one hub;*
2   *On its non-being depends the usefulness of the wheel.*
3   *You make a vessel, kneading clay;*
4   *On its non-being depends the usefulness of the vessel.*
5   *You make a room, carving out doors and windows;*
6   *On its non-being depends the usefulness of the room.*
7   *Therefore, being's advantage*
8   *Is non-being's usefulness.*

Probably "non-being" is one of the most abstract terms in any language. Nonetheless, we seem to understand perfectly well what is meant by the "non-being" (*wu*) of such mundane things as the hub of a wheel, a vessel and a room—certainly, no less than what is meant by their "being" (*yu*). I read this chapter, taking these two terms in their naive sense.

Obviously, the non-being of things is not amenable to our sense perception. Perhaps, it is for this reason that we see things primarily from the perspective of being. Things are beings; there are no non-beings. But there cannot be beings where there are no non-beings. Lao Tzu has already declared: "Being and non-being rise together" (Ch. 2). In this chapter, he is reminding us of the correlative nature of "being" and "non-being," thus rejecting our lopsided perspective of "being."

The last two lines read: "Therefore being's advantage/ Is non-being's usefulness." One may be tempted to read this statement in an abstract sense, taking "non-being" to refer to Tao and "being" to the world of beings. But such a reading is unwarranted. Here Lao Tzu is simply drawing a general conclusion from the previous lines, though I grant that by pointing to "non-being's advantage," he is trying to release us from our perspective of "being" and open our eyes to what is beyond the visible.

CHAPTER 12

1   *The five colors make man's eyes go blind.*
2   *The five tones make man's ears go deaf.*
3   *The five tastes injure man's palate.*
4   *Hunting on horseback*
5   *Makes man's mind go crazy.*
6   *Rare goods*
7   *Impede man's action.*
8   *That is why the sage*
9   *Cares for the stomach, not for the eye.*
10 *Therefore he discards that and takes this.*

Humans lose the inborn capacities of their faculties, by attaching themselves to such values of civilization as the "five colors"[1] the "five tones,"[2] and the "five tastes,"[3] thus neglecting their body's life. Unlike them, the sage "cares for the stomach, not for the eye." Once again, the primacy of bodily existence.

The phrase "discard that and take this"[4] in the last line is a set phrase, indicating a rejection of one thing in favor of another. The same line reappears twice later.

Notes

[1]   The "five colors" are green, yellow, red, white, and black; they refer to beautiful sights.

[2]   The "five tones" are those of the Chinese musical scale; they refer to beautiful sounds.

41

Reading Lao Tzu

3 The "five tastes" are sweet, pungent, sour, salty, and bitter; they refer to the discrimination of tastes of food.

4 *Ch'ü pi ch'ü tz'u.*

42

CHAPTER 13

1   *"Be alarmed by favor and disgrace;*
2   *High rank brings you great misfortune, as if your own body. "¹*
3   *What is the meaning of "Be alarmed by favor and disgrace"?*
4   *Regard favor as low.*
5   *Be alarmed to receive it;*
6   *Be alarmed to lose it.*
7   *This is the meaning of "Be alarmed by favor and disgrace. "*
8   *What is the meaning of "High rank brings you great misfortune, as if your own body"?*
9   *My reason for having great misfortune*
10 *Is my having a body.*
11 *If I had no body,*
12 *What misfortune would I have?*
13 *Therefore, if a man values the care of his body above ruling all under Heaven,*
14 *He may be given all under Heaven.*
15 *If a man cherishes his body more than ruling all under Heaven,*
16 *All under Heaven may be entrusted to him.*

"Favor and disgrace" come from the ruler. Why should they alarm you? Because they make you an object of another man's whim; your life will no longer be yours.

There is no misfortune outside the body's life. Only the sage recognizes this elemental truth. Who else would value the care of his body more than ruling all under Heaven? Therefore, to the sage alone can the care of the people be entrusted.

Notes

[1]   The meaning of the first two lines is uncertain.

CHAPTER 14

1   *You look at it but don't see it.*
2   *So you name it the Invisible.*
3   *You listen to it but don't hear it.*
4   *So you name it the Inaudible.*
5   *You grasp at it but don't touch it.*
6   *So you name it the Intangible.*
7   *These three*
8   *Are beyond scrutiny.*
9   *Therefore, blend them into one.*
10   *No brightness above it,*
11   *No darkness below it—*
12   *Boundless, it cannot be named.*
13   *Return to the objectless object.*
14   *It is called the shapeless shape—*
15   *The formless form.*[1]
16   *It is called the vague and dim.*
17   *You meet it but don't see its head.*
18   *You follow it but don't see its back.*
19   *Hold on to the Tao of old,*
20   *And thereby ride the being of now.*
21   *Know the old beginning,*
22   *Which is called the thread of Tao.*

Tao is infinite; therefore it is "Invisible," "Inaudible," and "Intangible."

In lines 13-15, one reads three self-contradictory phrases: "objectless object" (*wu wu*), "shapeless shape" (*wu chuang*) and "formless form" (*wu hsiang*). By each of them, of course, Lao Tzu is referring to the infinite Tao. In the Chinese text, they

45

literally mean, respectively: "no object," "no shape," and "no form."[2]

The "Tao of old" in line 19 means the "constant Tao." Hold on to Tao, as you carry on your earthly existence today.

Again, the "old beginning"[3] in the penultimate line refers to Tao, as the phrase "the thread of Tao" in the next line indicates.[4]

Notes

[1]   The standard text has "objectless form" (*wu wu chih hsiang*) in place of "formless form."

[2]   In each case, the character *wu*, as a negative particle, precedes the word it negates. Recall the following line from Ch. 1: "By non-being [*wu*] you name the beginning of Heaven and Earth."

[3]   Recall the phrase "the beginning of Heaven and Earth" in Ch. 1.

[4]   The phrase "the thread of Tao" (*tao chi*) may be puzzling if one searches for its meaning literally. But a literal reading may be only misleading. Tao is the "undifferentiated" (Ch. 25) One, of which one cannot speak of different aspects. One translator renders *tao chi* as the "essence of Tao." (See Waley, p. 159.) However, there is no such thing as the "essence" of Tao, something to be distinguished from what is "accidental" to it. The addition of *chi* to *tao* in the text may have been simply rhetorical. In the original text, it should be noted, the character *chi* for "thread" does rhyme with the character *shih* for "beginning" in the preceding line. (See Fukunaga, Vol. 1, p. 114.) It is possible that by the phrase Lao Tzu intends to evoke a certain image—say, the image of Tao as that "thread" which runs through all ages or all beings. Still, one must say, *tao chi* can only refer to Tao, no more and no less than Tao.

CHAPTER 15

1   *Of old a man who practiced Tao[1] best*
2   *Had insight into the subtlest and penetrated into the*
     darkest.
3   *His depth was not to be plumbed.*
4   *Truly, because his depth was not to be plumbed,*
5   *He could be portrayed only arbitrarily:*
6   *Hesitant as if crossing a river in winter;*
7   *Cautious as if fearing all four sides;*
8   *Inviolable like a guest;*
9   *Loose like ice about to thaw;*
10   *Simple like the uncarved block;*
11   *Empty like a valley;*
12   *Murky like muddy water.*
13   *Who can be muddy and yet, keeping still, slowly turn clear?*
14   *Who can be calm and yet, keeping active, slowly come to*
     life?
15   *He who embraces this Tao*
16   *Never wishes to be full.*
17   *Truly, because he is never full,*
18   *He decays yet renews himself.* [2]

In this chapter Lao Tzu gives a poetic depiction of the man of
Tao. He begins with the phrase "of old," because *today's* man of
Tao is different from the man of Tao of antiquity. *Today's* man
of Tao follows the human way, the way of civilization, rather
than the way of nature.[3] He lives in the world of names. The true
man of Tao, however, lives in the nameless.

The man of Tao is "hesitant" and "cautious." In this he is no
different from all other creatures living in nature. And yet he is

47

"inviolable," because he holds onto Tao. He is "loose like ice about to thaw." He is carefree, knowing no inhibition. He is "simple like the uncarved block" (*p'u*). His mind is undifferentiated "like muddy water." Who can be "murky" yet "still" and "clear"? Who can be "calm" yet "active" and full of "life"? Only the man of Tao can. His desires come and go, as his body's needs rise and recede. But he is free of all wishes and ambitions. He is forever one with the life-process of Tao, where decay means renewal.

Keep in mind that this portrayal of the ancient man of Tao is "only arbitrary," as the poet prefaces it. Why "arbitrary"? Because it is a depiction in words of a man who lives namelessly, that is, beyond words.

A note on the term "uncarved block," which occurs frequently. *P'u* means wood not yet touched by human hands. By this image Lao Tzu means the state of being in nature, unaffected by human civilization.

Notes

[1] I follow the Ma-wang-tui Text B in reading *tao* in place of *shih*.

[2] The standard text has the negative particle *pu*, rather than the connective *erh*, before *hsin ch'eng* ("to renew"). I take it to be an error. See Fukunaga, Vol. 1, p. 125. One reads in Ch. 22: "To decay is to renew."

[3] Note that Tao for Confucius is the human way, as opposed to the way of nature. His *chün-tzu* ("noble man") is none other than the practitioner of the human way. Probably, Lao Tzu is here contrasting the man of Tao of antiquity with the Confucian "noble man." See Appendix I.

CHAPTER 16

1   *Attain the utmost emptiness,*
2   *Hold fast to stillness.*
3   *The ten thousand things rise together;*
4   *I see them return.*
5   *All things flourish;*
6   *Each reverts to its root.*
7   *Reverting to the root is called stillness.*
8   *It means submission to fate.*
9   *Submission to fate is called [submission to] the constant.*
10 *To know the constant is called enlightenment.*
11 *If you do not know the constant,*
12 *You act blindly, ruining yourself.*
13 *Knowing the constant, you will be all-embracing.*
14 *All-embracing, hence impartial;*
15 *Impartial, hence king;*
16 *King, hence Heaven;*
17 *Heaven, hence Tao;*
18 *Tao, hence long-lasting.*
19 *Thus, you will be free of danger until the end of your life.*

By "emptiness" (*hsü*) is meant the mind free of all ideas and desires. Thus, the opening line means the silencing of the mind's activity, which leads to "stillness" (*ching*). In absolute stillness, "I see" the ten thousand things rise, flourish and return to Tao. This "seeing" is pure awareness, free of all thoughts.

In line 7, Lao Tzu is stating, rather cryptically, the "still" return of the ten thousand things to their source. This return in "stillness" means "silent" (*ching*) submission to Tao, namely, to "fate."

Line 9 means the ten thousand things' obeying of the eternal process of Tao. Does one recognize the "constant"? To recognize it is to be "enlightened" (*ming*).[1] One who fails to recognize it "acts blindly"; he lives in the dark, endangering his life.

When you "know the constant," you are selfless. Hence, "all-embracing" and "impartial." You will thus be kingly and, indeed, be one with Heaven and Tao.

Notes

[1]   See Appendix II.

CHAPTER 17

1   *Of the rulers, the best is one of whose existence his people*
    are [merely] aware;
2   *Next comes one whom they love and praise;*
3   *Next comes one whom they fear;*
4   *Next comes one whom they despise.*
5   *When you don't trust them,*
6   *They will not trust you.*
7   *Calm, I rarely speak.*[1]
8   *Yet the task is accomplished;*
9   *The people call me* tzu-jan.

The sage rules without ruling (*wu-wei*). Therefore, the people
are merely aware of his existence. They think everything is
happening *of itself. Tzu-jan* (literally "to be so of itself") means
"to be so by nature."[2]In this sense, *tzu-jan* is the *way* things are in
and by nature. As a substantive, however, it may be taken to
mean the *world* as it is in and by nature. It is in this substantive
sense that it comes close to what we commonly mean by the
word "nature" by itself (that is, not idiomatically, with "by" or
"in").

The people are right when they believe that things happen
to them by nature (*tzu-jan*) under the sage's rule. For he indeed
"does nothing" (*wu-wei*). His doing is nature's doing, which
is at the same time Tao's doing. Here one may recognize the
mutual implication of the ideas of *wu-wei*, Tao, and *tzu-jan*—
all of which the sage represents.

The sage trusts his people, as he trusts Tao. Why must he
speak? "*Tzu-jan* rarely speaks" (Ch. 23).

Notes

[1] As is often the case, this line has no subject in the original text. But I provide "I" as the subject of the sentence, in view of the closing line.

[2] See Graham, pp. 190 and 226.

CHAPTER 18

1   *When the great Tao is abandoned,*
2   *You have humaneness and righteousness.*
3   *When wisdom appears,*
4   *You have great falsehood.*
5   *When the six relations are in disharmony,*
6   *You have filial piety and parental love.*
7   *When the state is in disorder,*
8   *You have loyal ministers.*

The Confucians teach the virtues of "humaneness" (*jen*), "righteousness" (*i*), "wisdom" (*chih*), "filial piety" (*hsiao*), "parental love" (*tz'u*) and "loyalty" (*chung*).[1] For them, to be truly human is to recognize and practice these virtues. But Lao Tzu finds in these Confucian ideas nothing but man's abandoning of Tao.[2]

By "great falsehood" (*ta wei*)[3] Lao Tzu means the false flowering of human intelligence, namely, human civilization. Civilization is "false," because it is contrary to Tao: it suppresses life in the name of universal happiness. It pursues the way of force: it brings war in the name of peace, violence in the name of order, and oppression in the name of justice.

Seeking the human way, separate from Tao, man creates myriad institutions (names), such as conventions governing the family ("six relations"), regulations governing the state, and sacrificial rites for the deceased parents. These institutions only betray man's departure from Tao. Would you need "filial piety" and "parental love" when the family is in harmony, and "loyal ministers" when the state is in order?

Notes

1. Add "ritual propriety" (*li*) to this list. And you will have all the central ideas of Confucius. Lao Tzu's target is obvious.
2. See Appendix I.
3. The character *wei* (in *ta wei*) is composed of two parts: the radical component, *jen*, meaning "human," and the signifying component, *wei*, meaning "action"—their combination thus etymologically referring to "human action." This fact is revealing in that the formation of this ideogram suggests the equation of human action with falsehood.

CHAPTER 19

1 *Banish sagehood and wisdom,*
2 *And the people will benefit a hundredfold.*
3 *Banish humaneness and righteousness,*
4 *And the people will return to filial piety and parental love.*
5 *Banish cleverness and profit,*
6 *And there will be no more thieves and robbers.*
7 *These three*
8 *I take to be insufficient as maxims.*
9 *Therefore, let them be attached to the following:*
10 *Display plainness and embrace the uncarved block,*
11 *Diminish the self and reduce desires.*

Once again we read Lao Tzu's critique of human civilization. Notice, however, his mention of "sagehood" (*sheng*) along with "wisdom." It too should be banished because when you teach and praise *sheng*, you will turn it into one more source of contention, another name.

The root meaning of the character *su* for "plainness" is white raw silk before being dyed. Obviously, the sense of the *su* image is identical with that of the *p'u* image (of the "uncarved block."): they both point to the state of *tzu-jan*, being unaffected by human intervention or civilization. To display *su* and embrace *p'u* is to lead the life of *tzu-jan*, free of the desires and fancies of civilization. Note that the "self" (*szu*) (as opposed to the whole or the Other) arises with the arrival of civilization. To diminish it is to return to the state of the nameless Tao, *tzu-jan*.

CHAPTER 20

1   *Banish learning, and you will have no worries.*
2   *"Yes" and "yeah"—*
3   *How far apart are they?*
4   *Good and bad—*
5   *How far apart are they?*
6   *"What others fear*
7   *You must fear."*
8   *How outlandish! It will never end.*
9   *Everybody is cheerful,*
10 *As if enjoying a great feast;*
11 *As if going up to the terrace for the Spring Festival.*
12 *I alone am unexcited, giving no sign,*
13 *Like a baby who has not yet smiled;*
14 *Weary, as if nowhere to return.*
15 *Everybody has more than enough,*
16 *I alone seem dispossessed.*
17 *Mine is the mind of an ignorant man.*
18 *How indifferent!*
19 *Common folks are bright,*
20 *I alone am dark.*
21 *They are keen,*
22 *I alone am dull.*
23 *Adrift, I feel as if on the sea—*
24 *Blown by a high wind that seems never to come to rest.*
25 *Everybody is put to use,*
26 *I alone am stubborn and foolish like a boor.*
27 *Alone, different from others, I treasure the nursing mother.*

The proper way of reading this chapter is perhaps to read it as a poem, as Lao Tzu's song of himself. He sings of his profound solitude in the midst of the multitude that has left Tao.[1] His is the solitude of one who experiences an unbridgeable distance between himself and the rest of humanity. He feels alone in his awareness of the presence of the "nursing mother," Tao.

One may detect a certain irony in the poet's contrast of himself with the common folk. He is portraying himself precisely in the way he knows he appears in the eyes of the multitude.

Notes

[1]   The opening line seems out of place. A number of commentators have pointed out, on various grounds, that it should belong in the preceding chapter. See Chan (1963b), p. 135.

CHAPTER 21

1   *The look of the great Te*
2   *Follows from Tao alone.*
3   *It is Tao embodied.*
4   *How vague and dim it is!*
5   *Vague and dim—*
6   *In it are forms.*
7   *Vague and dim—*
8   *In it are things.*
9   *Deep and dark—*
10   *In it is the vital essence,*
11   *Which is most real.*
12   *In it is evidence.*
13   *From the time of old till today,*
14   *Its name has never departed.*
15   *By it you view the beginning of all.*
16   *How do I know the shape of the beginning of all?*
17   *By this.*

This chapter is Lao Tzu's song of "the mysterious female." I take the opening line[1] to be his subtle (perhaps, poetic) reference to "the gate of the mysterious female," the female organs.[2] The poet is describing the "look" (*yung*) of "the great Te of the hollow."[3] Hence, his visual language throughout.

"Deep and dark—/ In it is the vital essence [*ching*]." Lao Tzu is using here the word *ching* in its elemental sense: namely, the *seed* of life. The "gate of the mysterious female" is "Tao embodied"—"the root of Heaven and Earth."

Notes

[1] *K'ung te chih yung.*

[2] This chapter is almost universally read as one about Tao rather than about the "great Te" (*k'ung te*)—in spite of the opening line. I depart from this tradition.

[3] *K'ung te* may be rendered as "the Te of the hollow." The character *k'ung* means "hole" or "hollow" as well as "great." Hence, *k'ung te* may be read to have a double meaning of "the great Te of the hollow." My reading gives also a definite, concrete meaning to Lao Tzu's repeated use of the pronoun "it" in the chapter. Interestingly enough, it may be worth noting that Wang Pi, the man whose interpretation of this chapter has become the standard one, writes in the first sentence of his comment: "*K'ung* is emptiness" (*k'ung k'ung yeh*). Undoubtedly, he is reading the character to mean "hollow" rather than "great." However, he characteristically interprets it from his abstract, metaphysical level. With him *k'ung te* comes to mean the virtue (*te*) of "emptiness"—the state of mind with which the sage acts. I am taking its concrete meaning seriously.

CHAPTER 22

1   *To yield is to remain whole;*
2   *To bend is to get up straight;*
3   *To be hollow is to be full;*
4   *To decay is to renew;*
5   *To be small is to gain;*
6   *To have many is to be perplexed.*
7   *Therefore the sage,*
8   *Embracing the One, becomes the model for all under Heaven.*
9   *He does not show himself, therefore his presence is bright.*
10 *He does not claim to be right, therefore his virtue shines.*
11 *He is not boastful of his act, therefore his merit is great.*
12 *He is not conceited, therefore he is long-lasting.*
13 *Only because he does not contend,*
14 *No one under Heaven can contend with him.*
15 *Can the old saying "To yield is to remain whole"*
16 *Be an empty phrase?*
17 *Truly, he remains whole, and the world returns to him.*

In the first part (lines 1-6), one reads a series of aphorisms. Lao Tzu's meaning:

> Yield, so that you may not break;
> Bend, so that you may rise again;
> Be empty, so that you may be filled;
> Decay, so that you may be renewed;
> Be small, so that you may grow;
> Have little, so that you may not be perplexed.

Here he is teaching once again the female virtues of passivity and non-contention. Yielding, bending, hollowness, decaying, smallness, having little—all these are, however, precisely the sort of qualities that the male-dominant world despises.

In the second part (lines 7-14), Lao Tzu describes how the sage "becomes the model for all under Heaven." Notice his paradoxical logic once again. The sage is neither ostentatious, nor self-righteous, nor self-important, nor contentious. Precisely because of this, "his presence is "bright," "his virtue shines," "his merit is great," "he is long-lasting," and "no one under Heaven can contend with him." On the other hand, the ambitious and the vain fail to achieve what they seek, precisely because of their self-seeking acts.

CHAPTER 23

1   Tzu-jan *rarely speaks.*
2   *Therefore no windstorm lasts all morning;*
3   *No rainstorm lasts all day.*
4   *Who causes these things?*
5   *Heaven and Earth.*
6   *If even Heaven and Earth can cause nothing to last forever,*
7   *How could man?*
8   *Therefore those who follow Tao*
9   *Are one with Tao.*
10   *Those who attain Te are one with Te;*
11   *Those who lose [Te] are one with the loss.*
12   *When a man is one with Tao,*
13   *Tao also rejoices at gaining him;*
14   *When a man is one with Te,*
15   *Te also rejoices at gaining him.*
16   *When a man is one with the loss,*
17   *The loss also rejoices at gaining him.*
18   *When you don't trust others,*
19   *They will not trust you.*

In lines 1-7, Lao Tzu speaks of the silence of nature (*tzu-jan*). But one may hear between the lines his other voice: his critique of humanity that never stops "speaking." Nature does not speak, but there is the never-ending noise of human civilization. Speaking, we humans make friends and enemies; speaking, we discourse, argue, plot, insult, deceive, threaten, quarrel and so on. Thus we have our tumultuous world. But, of course, all these human noises sooner or later vanish, and nature's silence returns. Can one hear the silence of eternity? To hear it is to return to the nameless.

I find the rest of the chapter altogether unintelligible. In fact, there exist significantly different versions of many of these lines,[1] which would make any reading of it at best tentative.[2]

Notes

[1] See Fukunaga, Vol. 1, pp. 179-181. See also Henricks (1989), pp. 234-235.

[2] It is quite possible that in this part Lao Tzu originally played with words, but some literally-minded interpreters tampered with it, in their attempts to make sense of the passage.

CHAPTER 24

1   *He who tiptoes cannot remain standing;*
2   *He who strides cannot travel;*
3   *He who shows himself has no bright presence;*
4   *He who claims to be right does not shine;*
5   *The boastful have no merit;*
6   *The conceited do not last long.*
7   *From Tao's standpoint*
8   *Such things may be called excess food and superfluous action.*
9   *Creatures abhor them.*
10   *Therefore the man of Tao stays away from them.*

What kind of act is "tiptoeing" or "striding"? They are attempts to "extend" oneself beyond one's inborn capacities. In that sense, they are *self*-extending, going against one's nature (*tzu-jan*). Self-extending acts exist only in the human world. In the first two lines, Lao Tzu points out the futility of such acts. The ambitious are those who try to extend themselves against nature.

Earlier in Chapter 22, we read the following lines describing the sage's selfless life of *wu-wei*: "He does not show himself, therefore his presence is bright./ He does not claim to be right, therefore his virtue shines./ . . . ." We now read in lines 3-6 the obverse of those lines. The ambitious, the self-righteous, and the self-important fail to obtain what they seek *because* of their ever self-conscious, self-extending acts. Such acts are "excess food and superfluous action." They are products of human civilization. Where would one find "excess food" or "superfluous action" in nature?

64

CHAPTER 25

1　*There is something undifferentiated*
2　*That precedes the birth of Heaven and Earth.*
3　*Silent and still,*
4　*It stands by itself and never changes—*
5　*All-pervading and never in danger.*
6　*One may regard it as the mother of Heaven and Earth.*[1]
7　*I don't know its proper name;*
8　*I address it as Tao.*
9　*Were I forced to name it, I would call it Great.*
10　*"Great" means "to go."*
11　*"To go" means "far away."*
12　*"Far away" means "to return."*
13　*Therefore Tao is great,*
14　*Heaven is great,*
15　*Earth is great,*
16　*The king is also great.*
17　*In the universe there are four greats.*
18　*King is one of them.*
19　*The measure for man is Earth;*
20　*The measure for Earth is Heaven;*
21　*The measure for Heaven is Tao;*
22　*The measure for Tao is* tzu-jan.

One may be tempted to read the opening two lines as a statement of a necessary truth: namely, that what precedes the differentiated (Heaven and Earth) must necessarily be "something undifferentiated." But Lao Tzu is not asserting a vacuous tautology. What he says here is a statement of *existence*: "There *is* something undifferentiated . . . ." One may ask, What sort of existence is it? But that would be a wrong question. For it is "undifferentiated," and what is "undifferentiated" is nameless.

So Lao Tzu confesses: "I don't know its proper name." Yet he continues: "I address it as Tao./ Were I forced to name it, I would call it Great." These lines reveal his awareness of the paradox of speaking of the unspeakable, the paradox of the *Tao Te Ching* itself.

In the next nine lines (10-18), Lao Tzu first lays down what "Great" means, by a soritic chain of propositions, before proceeding to announce the "four greats." How are we to read these lines, which seem rather esoteric or arbitrary? I propose to read them as Lao Tzu's poetic excursion. (It would be futile to attempt an analytic reading of the passage, whether metaphysically or empirically.)

The last four lines reflect the ancient Chinese cosmological hierarchy: Heaven above Earth, and Earth above humans. By proclaiming Tao as "the measure for Heaven," Lao Tzu is once again going beyond that old cosmology.

The last line says: "The measure for Tao is *tzu-jan*." This, of course, does not mean that *tzu-jan* exists somehow over and above Tao. Tao is *tzu-jan*, and *tzu-jan* is Tao. The line may be rendered as: "The measure for Tao is to be so of itself [*tzu-jan*]."

Notes

[1] The standard text has "all under Heaven" (*t'ien hsia*) in place of "Heaven and Earth" (*t'ien ti*). But the Mawant-tui Texts have the latter.

CHAPTER 26

1   *The heavy is the root of the light;*
2   *Stillness is the lord of bustle.*
3   *Therefore the prince,*[1]
4   *Traveling all day,*
5   *Never parts with his baggage-wagon.*
6   *Even at a magnificent sight,*
7   *He remains at ease, unmoved.*
8   *How could the lord of ten thousand chariots*
9   *Regard his own body more lightly than all under Heaven?*
10 *If you act lightly, the root is lost;*
11 *If you bustle, the lord is lost.*

One finds in this chapter two parallel pairs of contrasting words: "heavy" (*chung*) versus "light" (*ch'ing*), and "stillness" (*ching*) versus "bustle" (*tsao*). "Heavy" and "still" is one who never parts with Tao; "light" and "bustling" is one who pursues names.

Once again, Lao Tzu speaks of the primacy of the body's life: Cherish your body more than ruling all under Heaven! (Notice an irony in lines 8-9.) The ruler's[2] body is "heavier" (*chung*) than all under Heaven, not because he is a ruler (which is nothing but a name), but because the body's life is real whereas rulership is not.

Notes

[1]   Read *chün-tzu* in place of *sheng jen*.

[2]   The "lord of ten thousand chariots" originally meant only the "Son of Heaven"—the ruler of all under Heaven. But it later came to mean also the

ruler of a powerful state during the Warring States period. "Chariot" here means a military vehicle.

Chapter 27

1   *Perfect going leaves no tracks.*
2   *Perfect speech has no flaws.*
3   *Perfect counting uses no counters.*
4   *The perfect lock uses no bolt; it is impossible to open.*
5   *The perfect knot uses no rope; it is impossible to untie.*
6   *Therefore the sage*
7   *Is always perfect in delivering people from distress.*
8   *Thus he abandons no one.*
9   *He is always perfect in delivering creatures from distress.*
10   *Thus he abandons no creature.*
11   *This is called following the light.*
12   *Therefore the perfect man*
13   *Is the leader of the imperfect man;*
14   *The imperfect man*
15   *Is the asset of the perfect man.*
16   *He who does not treasure his leader,*
17   *He who does not cherish his asset,*
18   *Though he may be wise, is greatly deluded.*
19   *This is called the fundamental secret.*

In the first five lines we read a succession of aphorisms characteristic of Lao Tzu's style. How can any "going" "leave no tracks"? What kind of "speech" would be "flawless"? "Counting" without using "counters"? "Locking" without a "bolt"? Making a "knot" without a "rope"? But does the sun leave tracks as it travels the sky? Does the moon count the days of the month with counters as it keeps its nightly appointments? Haven't you heard the flawless message of your body? Does nature ever use a bolt to lock, or a rope to tie a knot? And yet, you can never open what nature locks, nor untie what it ties. What do these "perfect" acts have in common? They are all Tao's working—the spontaneous acts of *tzu-jan*. "Perfect going" is no-going, "perfect speech" no-speech, "perfect counting" no-counting, and so on. They involve no (human) intentionality; they are acts of *wu-wei*.

Such are acts of the sage in "delivering people [and creatures] from distress." He "abandons" none, as he rules selflessly, following Tao. Therefore, Lao Tzu calls his acts of *wu-wei* "[acts] following the light [*hsi ming*]."[1]

Turning to the rest of the chapter (lines 12-19), one may find its connection with the preceding lines unclear, though its meaning may not be hard to follow. I read this part as a statement of the equality of "perfect man" and "imperfect man." They are equal under the aspect of Tao.

Notes

[1] See Appendix II.

CHAPTER 28

1   *He¹ knows the male,*
2   *Yet holds fast to the female,*
3   *And thus becomes the ravine of all under Heaven.*
4   *When he becomes the ravine of all under Heaven,*
5   *The constant Te will never desert him.*
6   *He returns to the baby.*
7   *He knows white,*
8   *Yet holds fast to black,*
9   *And thus becomes the model for all under Heaven.*
10 *When he becomes the model for all under Heaven,*
11 *The constant Te will never fail him.*
12 *He returns to the infinite.*
13 *He knows glory,*
14 *Yet holds fast to ignominy,*
15 *And thus becomes the valley of all under Heaven.*
16 *When he becomes the valley of all under Heaven,*
17 *His constant Te will be sufficient,*
18 *He returns to the uncarved block.*
19 *When the uncarved block scatters, it turns into vessels.*
20 *When the sage uses them,*
21 *He becomes chief of ministers.*
22 *Therefore great cutting does not split.*

I read this chapter (through line 18) as a three-stanza poem in praise of the sage.² Lao Tzu sings of the sage's "constant Te" that "will never desert him." How does he attain this Te? By "knowing the male/ yet holding fast to the female," by "knowing white/ yet holding fast to black," and by "knowing glory/ yet holding fast to ignominy."

In reading this poem, let us keep in mind three pairs of opposites: "male"/"female," "white"/"black"[3] and "glory"/ "ignominy." They represent the value-universe of ancient China, where the first of each pair was prized, and the second despised. The sage "knows" this man-made universe better than anyone else, yet rejects it from the nameless perspective of Tao. So he "holds fast to" what the whole world disdains. What is lowly in the human eyes is "near to Tao"[4]; it represents the nameless in the human universe of names.[5]

It is, of course, not that "holding fast to" the lowly ("female," "black" and "ignominy") is the same thing as "holding fast to" the nameless Tao. Rather, by "holding fast" to the lowly, one overcomes the very opposition of what is praiseworthy and what is despicable, and may thus return to the nameless, to Tao. Note how each of the three stanzas ends:

> And you will return to the baby;
> And you will return to the infinite;
> And you will return to the uncarved block.

So far we have read this chapter (through line 18) as Lao Tzu's song of the sage's "constant Te." However, I should note, the poem may be read, at the same time, as his call for a transvaluation of the male-dominant universe of ancient China, where the male was believed to be not only strong but also intelligent ("white") and praiseworthy ("glory"), and the female not only weak but also ignorant ("black") and despicable ("ignominy"). This call may indeed be hard to miss especially when the same lines are given the following alternative rendering: (I give here only the first stanza. The next two should follow the same pattern.)

> Know the male,
> Hold fast to the female,
> And you will become the ravine of all under Heaven.

When you become the ravine of all under Heaven,
The constant Te will never desert you,
And you will return to the baby.[6]

Turning to the last four lines, the uncarved block "scatters" when one "cuts" (*chih*) it into various artifacts. So the One—the original unity of the nameless—"scatters" when man differentiates it by names. When this "scattering" occurs, people are now turned into diverse "vessels," each with a particular function. When the ruler[7] "uses" his people as "vessels," he does so as "chief of ministers."[8] But the sage does not "use" the people, as he rules without ruling. Under his rule, indeed, all "return to the uncarved block." Hence, "great cutting" is no-cutting; it "does not split."[9]

Notes

[1]   The Chinese text has no grammatical subject in lines 1-18 where "He" (or "he") is provided as the subject of a clause in my translation. The pronoun refers to the sage.

[2]   Perhaps, one may easily recognize, even in translation, the identical pattern of six lines repeating three times. In the Chinese text, each stanza has the same number of characters (3, 3, 4, 4, 5) except for the last line in the third stanza. Notice the recurrence of the words "all under Heaven" (*t'ien-hsia*) and "constant Te" (*ch'ang te*) as well as the repetition of the form "He knows (*chih*) . . . ,/ Yet holds fast to (*shou*) . . . ." In the original text, the lines are all in rhyme. See Fukunaga, Vol. 1, p. 208.

[3]   The opposition of "white" and "black" refers to that of "intelligent" and "ignorant." See Fukunaga, Vol. 1, p. 211.

[4]   Recall the following lines in Ch. 8: "The supreme good is like water./ Water benefits the ten thousand things, but contends with nothing./ It dwells where everyone is loathe to be./ That is why it is near to Tao."

[5]   It is this "holding fast to" the lowly that Lao Tzu means by the line "[The sage/Tao] identifies with the dust" (*t'ung ch'i ch'en*). (The "dust," of course, means what is lowly or despicable.) This line appears twice, in Chs. 4 and 56, but its meaning seems generally misunderstood or lost to the reader. In both occurrences, the line has no grammatical subject in the Chinese text.

In my translation, I supply as its subject "Tao" in Ch. 4 and "The sage" in Ch. 56.

6 See Lau's translation in Lau, p. 85. This rendering is perfectly plausible in view of the fact that the original text has no grammatical subject.

7 The subject of this line in the Chinese text is *sheng jen* ("sage"). I take it that this word is used here simply in the sense of "wise ruler," in conformity with common usage, without meaning specifically Lao Tzu's ideal ruler, who rules through no-action. For instance, the Confucian *sheng jen* could satisfy the description of "sage" as "chief of ministers," but not Lao Tzu's. See Fukunaga, Vol. 1, p. 213.

8 I follow Fukunaga' reading. See Fukunaga, Vol. 1, p. 213.

9 As Waley notes, there is a word play here on the character *chih*, which also means "to rule." "Great cutting" means "great rule." See Waley, p. 178n.

CHAPTER 29

1   *Do you wish to conquer all under Heaven and rule it?*
2   *I see you will never succeed.*
3   *All under Heaven is a sacred vessel;*
4   *No one can rule it by action.*
5   *Whoever rules it by action destroys it;*
6   *Whoever seizes it loses it.*
7   *Therefore, among the creatures,*
8   *Some go, some follow;*
9   *Some breathe lightly, some blow hard;*
10 *Some are strong, some are weak;*
11 *Some break, some fall.*
12 *Therefore the sage*
13 *Shuns extremes,*
14 *Shuns extravagance,*
15 *Shuns vanity.*

All under Heaven is "sacred"; it belongs to Tao alone. Human action (*wu-wei*) violates it. Therefore, "whoever seizes [*chih*] it loses it."

What is to govern "by action"? It is to subject all under Heaven to the ruler's personal will. But all living beings are different by nature. Some lead, some follow. Some breathe heavily, some softly. Do you wish to make them all behave in the same way, by decree or force? You will only fail. Life suppressed is life destroyed.

"Extremes," "extravagance," and "vanity" are all products of civilization. Therefore, the sage rejects them.

CHAPTER 30

1   *He who assists the ruler by Tao*
2   *Does not resort to arms to dominate all under Heaven by force.*
3   *This thing loves to rebound.*
4   *Where troops have encamped,*
5   *Brambles grow;*
6   *After the raising of great armies*
7   *A famine follows invariably.*
8   *A good man merely lets it bear fruit;*
9   *He does not seek to force it.*
10 *He lets it bear fruit; he is not vainglorious.*
11 *He lets it bear fruit; he is not boastful.*
12 *He lets it bear fruit; he is not arrogant.*
13 *He lets it bear fruit, out of necessity.*
14 *He lets it bear fruit and does not force it.*
15 *When a thing reaches its prime, it becomes old.*
16 *Forcing is called contrary to Tao.*
17 *What is contrary to Tao expires early.*

In the previous chapter, we have seen Lao Tzu speak of the futility of any attempt to conquer all under Heaven by action. Here he is explicit in rejecting the use of arms and force.

Force necessarily invites counter-force: it "loves to rebound." The modern reader may be able to appreciate the validity of this statement, perhaps better than the ancients did, thanks to our "scientific" understanding of the human as well as the physical universe. Today, we tend to view not only natural but also human events in terms of the workings of force/counter-force or action/ reaction. As I write this comment, I cannot resist referring to the cycle of violence that has been going on between the Israelis and the Palestinians in their troubled land for nearly two years. What would we mean by "cycle of violence" if not action/reaction of force?

How sadly true is also that: "Where troops have encamped,/ Brambles grow;/ After the raising of great armies/ A famine follows invariably"! Perhaps these scenes are almost idyllic, compared with the enormity of human suffering and devastation of land that modern warfare brings upon us.

Heaven and Earth "let [all things] bear fruit" (*kuo*).[1] So does the sage. "Bearing fruit" is life's way. When a thing "bears fruit," it decays. Do not "force" (*ch'iang*) it. "Forcing" is to interfere with nature's process; it is contrary to Tao.

Notes

[1] The character *kuo* appears six times. Its root meaning is "fruit." Because of the uncertainty of Lao Tzu's meaning, however, it has been read variously. My reading is based on its root meaning; I interpret it as the opposite of "forcing" (*ch'iang*).

CHAPTER 31

1   *Dazzling arms*
2   *Are instruments of ill omen.*
3   *All creatures detest them.*
4   *Therefore the man of Tao does not keep company with them.*
5   *At home, the prince honors the left;*
6   *At war, the right.*
7   *Arms*
8   *Are instruments of ill omen—*
9   *No instruments for the prince.*
10   *When necessary to use them,*
11   *It's best to do so in calm disinterestedness.*
12   *You do not celebrate a victory.*
13   *To celebrate a victory*
14   *Is to delight in the slaughter of people.*
15   *He who delights in the slaughter of people*
16   *Will never realize his ambition under Heaven.*
17   *At times of good fortune, you honor the left;*
18   *At times of misfortune, you honor the right.*
19   *The second in command stands on the left;*
20   *The supreme commander stands on the right.*
21   *This means they stand as if observing funeral rites.*
22   *Having committed mass killings,*
23   *Let us weep with deep sorrow;*
24   *For a victory, let us observe funeral rites.*

Arms are "dazzling" (*chia*) to the lovers of power, as beautiful faces are to the lovers of beauty.[1] But they are "instruments of ill omen," which all living beings shun. They are instruments of death. Human power is nothing if not power to destroy.

Lines 10-11 do not imply that one may be able to use arms "in calm disinterestedness." I read them as a critique of *that* state of mind with which the war-going prince in fact uses arms. By "calm disinterestedness" Lao Tzu means the state of "emptiness" (*hsü*), devoid of all habits of mind such as hatred, vengeance, vindictiveness, and arrogance—the state of mind that only the man of *wu-wei* is capable of.

In ancient China, the place of honor was the left on occasion of good fortune, and the right on occasion of misfortune. Lines 5-6 and 17-21 refer to this practice. The prince honors the right at war, because it is an occasion of misfortune. For the same reason, "The supreme commander stands on the right."[2]

War is "the slaughter of people." But the civilized no longer see this. So they march on to the battlefield to kill. Winning, they celebrate killings, rather than mourn the dead. How has this state of affairs come about? Through man's pursuit of power over life.

Notes

[1] Notice the parallel between *chia ping* ("beautiful arms") and *chia jen* ("beautiful woman").

[2] See Fukunaga, Vol. 1, p. 229.

CHAPTER 32

1 *Tao is forever nameless.*
2 *Though the uncarved block is small,*
3 *No one under Heaven can make it his subject.*
4 *If kings and princes hold fast to it,*
5 *The ten thousand things will submit of their own accord;*
6 *Heaven and Earth will unite to send sweet dew;*
7 *The people will be fair of themselves, without being ordered.*
8 *When the cutting begins, names come to be.*
9 *As soon as names appear,*
10 *Know that it's time to stop.*
11 *By knowing this, you will be free from danger.*
12 *To draw an analogy, the working of Tao under Heaven*
13 *Is like streams and rapids flowing into great rivers and seas.*

The "uncarved block" (*p'u*) is "small"—that is, nameless—in the eyes of civilized man. But it belongs to no man. Even the Son of Heaven cannot subjugate it.

Let the ruler return to the nameless state of *p'u*. If he does, all under Heaven will "submit [to him] of their own accord"; Heaven and Earth will "send sweet dew"; and the people will be in harmony "without being ordered."

The word "cutting" (*chih*) has appeared before.[1] By this Lao Tzu is here referring to man's differentiation of the nameless through naming. "As soon as names appear,/ Know that it's time to stop." It's time to return to the nameless.

In the last two lines, Lao Tzu is stating that the ten thousand things ultimately return to their source, as all streams and rivers inevitably flow to the sea.

Notes

[1]   See my comment on Ch. 28.

CHAPTER 33

1 *He who knows others is wise;*
2 *He who knows himself is enlightened.*
3 *He who overcomes others has strength;*
4 *He who overcomes himself is strong.*
5 *He who knows to be content is rich.*
6 *He who persists in his action is strong-willed.*
7 *He who does not lose his place is long-lasting.*
8 *He who dies but does not perish is long-lived.*

Here we have a collection of aphorisms that may have come from more than one source. Lines 1-5 may indeed have come from Taoist sources, but even some of them (e.g., lines 3-5) could have been easily found in Confucian literature as well. The remaining lines definitely sound more Confucian than Taoist, as I shall note below.

Let us briefly read the first five aphorisms from a Taoist perspective. What is it to "know oneself"? It is to recognize that from which one comes and to which one returns: namely, Tao. One who "overcomes himself" is one who returns to his oneness with Tao, by overcoming his separateness. One who is "content" lacks nothing; therefore, he is "rich."

The last three lines resist any Taoist reading. The idea of "persisting in one's action [*wei*]" is clearly alien to Lao Tzu's teaching of no-action (*wu-wei*). A "strong-willed" person is one who is relentless in pursuing his set goal. Such a person evokes the counter image of Lao Tzu's "yielding" and "bending" female. The man of no-action has no fixed mind. The idea of keeping one's "place" is essential to the Confucian vision of hierarchical social order in the name-mediated world. One's "place" would be the place where one *ought to be*. But there is no such "place" in the nameless realm of nature.

The last aphorism would make perfect sense in Confucian terms, but not according to Lao Tzu's teachings. For the Confucians "he who dies but does not perish" would be one whose "name" survives his death. Such a one would be, for example, a minister who dies out of his loyalty to his prince, so that his "name" will live on. But "name" is the last thing that would concern Lao Tzu. After all, what would it mean "not to perish" after death, in his naturalistic universe? For him there is no life beyond the body's. When you die, you "revert to the root" (Ch. 16).

CHAPTER 34

1   *The great Tao overflows left and right,*
2   *The ten thousand things depend on it for their lives, and it never disowns them.*
3   *Its work is done, but it has no name.*
4   *It clothes and nurtures the ten thousand things, yet it makes no claim to be lord over them.*
5   *It is always free of desire.*
6   *It may be called small.*
7   *The ten thousand things return to it, yet it makes no claim to be lord over them.*
8   *It may be called great.*
9   *Because it never regards itself as great,*
10   *It can accomplish its greatness.*

The opening line evokes the image of Tao sweeping everywhere "left and right" like a cosmic deluge. There is nothing in the whole universe that escapes the sweep of Tao.

In lines 2, 3, 4, and 7, Lao Tzu describes Tao's work essentially in the same language as he depicts the work of the sage in Chapter 2. The sage's work is Tao's, and Tao's work is the sage's. Such is the "mysterious Te."

Tao is "always free of desire." It is selfless. Therefore, it is "small." At the same time, it is also "great," exactly for the same reason. To be truly great is to be small, to be selfless.

The ten thousand things submit to Tao, but it "makes no claim to be lord over them." That is why Tao is "great." Do you seek to be truly great? Make no claim over your people. They will submit to you of their own accord.

CHAPTER 35

1   *Holding fast to the great form,*
2   *Go anywhere under Heaven.*
3   *Wherever you go, nothing will harm you—*
4   *You will be safe and in peace.*
5   *Music and fine food*
6   *Make the passing stranger stop.*
7   *When Tao comes out from the mouth,*
8   *How flavorless it is!*
9   *You look at it, but it is invisible.*
10   *You listen to it, but it is inaudible.*
11   *You use it, but it is inexhaustible.*

"The great form" refers to Tao, the infinite.[1] How can anything or anyone "harm" you when you "go" "holding fast to" Tao? Note that the character for "to go" (*hsing*) also means "to conduct oneself." We have read in Chapter 14: "Hold on to the Tao of old,/ And thereby ride the being of now."

Tao is "invisible" and "inaudible." How "flavorless" is Tao-talk!

Notes

[1]   Recall the phrase "formless form" in Ch. 14. The "great form" (*ta hsiang*) is "formless" (*wu hsiang*). See my comment on Ch. 14.

CHAPTER 36

1 *When you want to shrink it,*
2 *You must first stretch it.*
3 *When you want to make it weak,*
4 *You must first make it strong.*
5 *When you want to make it fall,*
6 *You must first make it rise.*
7 *When you want to rob it,*
8 *You must first give it.*
9 *This is called subtle light.*
10 *The soft and weak prevails over the hard and strong.*
11 *The fish may not leave the depths.*
12 *The sharp instrument of the state*
13 *May not be shown to the people.*

Except for the last three lines, this chapter is quite straightforward. In the first eight lines, Lao Tzu warns the strong, the prosperous and the rich of the inevitable reversal of fortune.

> When Heaven is about to shrink you, it first stretches you.
> When Heaven is about to make you weak, it first makes you strong.
> When Heaven is about to make you fall, it first makes you rise.
> When Heaven is about to rob you, it first gives you.[1]

Such is the paradoxical logic of Tao.[2] To recognize it is to see "subtle light." However, few recognize it. So the strong think they will forever remain strong; the prosperous think they will forever remain prosperous, and so on. But their fortunes will be reversed sooner or later. "Turning back is Tao's motion" (Ch. 40).

Thus, "The soft and weak prevails over the hard and strong." Note that the prevailing of the weak over the strong means the prevailing of no-action (*wu-wei*) over action (*wei*). That is how the female prevails over the male, and how "the softest under Heaven [water]/ Rides roughshod over the hardest" (Ch. 43). This does not mean that no-action somehow *defeats* action. No-action (*wu-wei*) does nothing. Rather, it is in the transitory nature of every action (*wei*) that it passes away, and, with its passing, nature (*tzu-jan*) returns.

The meaning of the last three lines is uncertain. One can only speculate as to the meaning of the phrase "the sharp instrument of the state." There are various interpretations of the passage, none of which seems convincing.[3]

Notes

[1]   It may be noted that the original text has no subject in the first eight lines; in my translation I have supplied "you" merely as a sort of place-holder. The substitution of "you" for "Heaven" may well be justified particularly in view of the historical context in which Lao Tzu was writing: he was addressing the readership who believed in the will of Heaven as the controlling power of human fortune.

[2]   Recall the following lines from Ch. 22: "To yield is to preserve oneself whole;/ To bend is to get up straight;/ To be hollow is to be full;/ To decay is to renew;/ To be small is to gain;/ To have many is to be perplexed."

[3]   It seems that the only plausible reading of the lines would have to be somehow along the interpretation given in the Legalist text, the *Han Fei Tzu*, which identifies "the sharp instruments of the state" to be "reward and punishment" (Ch. 21). This only suggests the possibility that the passage itself is a later addition by a Legalist's hand. (The *Han Fei Tzu* contains the earliest extant comments on the *Tao Te Ching*.) It may be noted that the Legalists (*fa chia*), one of the "One Hundred Schools" of the Warring States

period, looked at the business of government entirely from the standpoint of the interest of the ruler or the state. They may be regarded as the advocates of Realpolitik, whom Waley calls the "Realists." For *fa chia* and its relation with Taoism, see Waley, pp. 68-86.

CHAPTER 37

1   *Tao never does,*[1]
2   *Yet leaves nothing undone.*
3   *If kings and princes hold fast to this,*
4   *The ten thousand things will transform of themselves.*
5   *Should desires arise after transformation,*
6   *I shall calm them with the nameless, uncarved block.*
7   *The nameless, uncarved block*
8   *Brings desirelessness.*
9   *With desirelessness comes stillness,*
10   *And all under Heaven will be at peace by itself.*

In this chapter, Lao Tzu once again returns to the subject of the sage ruling without ruling. When the ruler rules through *wu-wei*, the people "will transform of themselves." But Lao Tzu continues: "Should desires arise after transformation,/ I shall calm them with the nameless, uncarved block." Does this mean that the people's "transformation" should turn them completely free of desires? Does it also imply that the state of *p'u* is one of utter "desirelessness"? Indeed, the latter part of the chapter seems to mean that only "desirelessness" (*pu yü*) will ultimately bring about a universal peace. But what sort of peace would this be if "desirelessness" meant the total absence of desires? How would it be different from the peace of the dead, rather than of the living?

I have already noted that every living being must have certain desires the fulfillment of which is necessary for its very existence. Such are clearly biological desires. The living universe would indeed be inconceivable apart from such desires. What sort of "desirelessness" does Lao Tzu then envision here? I take it to be the absence of abstract, name-mediated desires, which we may call the *mind*'s desires, as opposed to the body's desires.[2] Once so understood, "transformation" would mean not the absence of *all* desires but release only from man-made desires, and the state of *p'u* not a state of dead nature but a state of living nature.

In the penultimate line, one reads: "With desirelessness comes stillness [*ching*]." *Ching* here means the silencing of desires of the mind.[3] When the people are freed of all abstract desires, they will cease to be ambitious, contentious, and so on. Hence, "all under Heaven will be at peace by itself."

Notes

[1] *Wu-wei.*

[2] Recall the following lines from Ch. 3: "Therefore the sage, in governing the people,/ Makes their minds empty,/ Their stomachs full . . . ."

[3] See my comment on Ch. 16.

BOOK TWO

TE

CHAPTER 38

1   *The man of superior virtue [te] is not virtuous;*
2   *Therefore he has virtue.*
3   *The man of inferior virtue never fails to be virtuous;*
4   *Therefore he has no virtue.*
5   *A man of superior virtue never acts;*
6   *He seeks nothing through action.*
7   *A man of inferior virtue acts;*
8   *He seeks [virtue] through action.*
9   *A man of superior humaneness [jen] acts;*
10   *Yet he seeks nothing through action.*
11   *A man of superior righteousness [i] acts;*
12   *He seeks [righteousness] through action.*
13   *A man of superior ritual propriety [li] acts;*
14   *And when others fail to respond accordingly,*
15   *He stretches his arm and charges at them.*
16   *Therefore, when Tao is lost, virtue appears;*
17   *When virtue is lost, humaneness appears;*
18   *When humaneness is lost, righteousness appears;*
19   *When righteousness is lost, ritual propriety appears.*
20   *Truly, ritual propriety means*
21   *The thinning of loyalty and truthfulness,*
22   *And the origin of disorder.*
23   *Foresight*
24   *Is the flower of Tao,*
25   *The beginning of folly.*
26   *Therefore the great man*
27   *Dwells in the thick,*
28   *Not in the thin,*
29   *In the fruit,*

30   *Not in the flower.*
31   *Therefore he discards that and takes this.*

In this chapter, Lao Tzu describes the genealogy of (Confucian) morals as the gradual fall of man from Tao. I have here translated *te* as "virtue" or "virtuous," instead of leaving it untranslated. This exception is made in view of the fact that Lao Tzu is here criticizing the Confucian notion of *te* as ethical virtue.[1] However, it may be noted, there is a constant shifting of the meaning of *te* between the Confucian "virtue" and Lao Tzu's Te (power of Tao), as he plays on the double meaning of *te*. The opening four lines may sound paradoxical, but they are not. One should be able to see this when one keeps in mind the shifting sense of the term *te* in the passage.

"Humaneness" (*jen*), "righteousness" (*i*), and "ritual propriety" (*li*) are three of the Confucian virtues.[2] It is revealing that Lao Tzu characterizes man of *jen* as one who "acts" (*wei*) but "seeks nothing," man of *i* as one who "acts" and "seeks [righteousness]," and man of *li* as one who not only "acts" but, also, demands that others "respond accordingly"—that is, "act" in some "proper" way. These are obviously all men of action (*wei*), who live in the world of names.

In lines 16-19, Lao Tzu states the successive stages of humanity's falling away from Tao. Perhaps one shouldn't attach too much importance to the sequence.[3] I find it interesting that he sees the beginning of the process in the appearance of virtue (*te*), that is, in the emerging of man's distinction between "virtuous" and "evil." This distinction, of course, signals the rise of moral consciousness, which means for Lao Tzu nothing other than man's separation from nature's way, his alienation from Tao.

Why is ritual propriety (*li*) "the thinning of loyalty and truthfulness"? Because man invents *rules* of propriety precisely when he can no longer count on fellow humans' "loyalty" and "truthfulness." In what way is ritual propriety the "origin of disorder"? Where there is no convention of propriety, there cannot be "disorder." In nature there exists neither "order" nor "disorder."

Lines 23-25. By "foresight" Lao Tzu refers to human wisdom (*chih*), another Confucian virtue. It is name-mediated wisdom, which is none other than the flowery appearance of Tao; it has nothing to do with Tao. With the pursuit of human wisdom begins the human "folly," the turning away from Tao.

Notice Lao Tzu's parallel use of two pairs of contrasting images in the last six lines. The "great man" discards what is "thin," the "flower of Tao," and takes what is "thick," the "fruit" of Tao.

Notes

1.   See Appendix I.
2.   See Appendix I.
3.   We have already read in Chapter 18: "When the great Tao is abandoned,/ You have humaneness [*jen*] and righteousness [*i*]." It may be worth noting that the sequence does coincide with the shifting emphasis in the early development of Confucianism: from *jen* (Confucius) to *i* (Mencius) and to *li* (Hsün Tzu). See Fukunaga, Vol. 2, p. 15.

Chapter 39

1   *The things of old that have attained the One:*
2   *Heaven, having attained the One, is clear;*
3   *Earth, having attained the One, is steady;*
4   *Spirits, having attained the One, possess their numinous power;*
5   *Valleys, having attained the One, are full;*
6   *The ten thousand things, having attained the One, come to life;*
7   *Kings and princes, having attained the One, become the model for All under Heaven.*
8   *It is by virtue of the One that they become what they are.*
9   *Were Heaven not clear by virtue of that,*
10   *I fear it would soon shatter;*
11   *Were Earth not steady by virtue of that,*
12   *I fear it would soon collapse;*
13   *Were spirits not to possess their numinous power by virtue of that,*
14   *I fear they would soon cease to be;*
15   *Were valleys not full by virtue of that,*
16   *I fear they would soon dry up;*
17   *Were the ten thousand things not to come to life by virtue of that,*
18   *I fear they would soon perish;*
19   *Were kings and princes not noble and high by virtue of that,*
20   *I fear they would soon fall.*
21   *Therefore, for the noble the humble is the root;*
22   *For the high the low is the foundation.*
23   *For this reason, kings and princes*

24   *Refer to themselves as "the orphaned one," "the widowed
      one," and "the ill-provided one."*
25   *Isn't this because the humble is the root?*
26   *Is it not?*
27   *Therefore, if you tally your honors you will count none.*
28   *Don't try to jingle like jade-bells,*
29   *Rather, sound like rolling rocks.*

The "One" is Tao, the source of all beings. All things are what
they are "by virtue of the One." Without the One, Heaven would
shatter, Earth would collapse, spirits would cease to be, valleys
would dry up, and the ten thousand things would become extinct.
And the universe would no longer be.

    What is the meaning of lines 21-26? The nobility depends on
the commoners for its existence; no peak soars into the sky
without its low base. But humans adore the "noble" and the
"high," and despise the "humble" and the "low." Such is the value-
universe of civilization. Lao Tzu calls for its inversion. Be a nameless
rock rolling on the hill, rather than a jade-bell hanging on the
rack.

CHAPTER 40

1   *Turning back is Tao's motion.*
2   *Being weak is Tao's function.*
3   *The ten thousand things under Heaven are born from being;*
4   *Being is born from non-being.*

What does Lao Tzu mean by "Tao's motion" in the laconic opening line? By that he means the way Tao operates in the phenomenal world. The phrase "turning back" (*fan*) here has a double meaning: it may be understood in the (intransitive) sense of "reverting" but also in the (transitive) sense of "causing (something) to revert."[1] In either case, the meaning amounts to the same. In the former case, it is every phenomenal thing that reverts to the opposite, whereas in the latter case, it is Tao that causes everything to revert to its opposite. Thanks to Tao's "turning back" motion, hot summer brings cool autumn; the living die; the rich become poor; empires rise and fall. This line, so understood, may sound like a platitude. (Are there after all things that do not "revert"?) All human strivings are, however, fundamentally attempts to counter "Tao's motion," and in the end, they all inevitably fail. We humans *act* (*wei*) to resist, put off, or dodge "Tao's motion."

As we turn to lines 3-4, I should like to have the reader recall our reading of the following lines in Chapter 1: "By non-being you name the beginning of Heaven and Earth;/ By being you name the mother of the ten thousand things." I read the present passage simply as a restatement of that earlier one. In the present chapter, Lao Tzu declares once again in terms of "being" (*yu*) and "non-being" (*wu*) the rise of the ten thousand things from Heaven and Earth, and of Heaven and Earth, in turn, from Tao.

One should keep in mind here that the passage in question

does not somehow imply that there is some *absolute* "non-being" (*wu*), out of which the whole universe of "being" (*yu*) arises. Yes, for Lao Tzu, Tao may be said to be absolute in some sense. But that does not mean that Tao *is* for him some *absolute* "non-being," which precedes the rise of "being(s)." The notion of "absolute non-being" has no meaning in Lao Tzu.[2] He is here asserting the rise of what *is* (namely, the finite universe) from what *is not* (namely, the infinite Tao). In so doing, he is *merely* making use of a pair of (correlative) names, "being" and "non-being."

Notes

[1] The Chinese character *fan* may also be read in both of these two senses.

[2] Recall the line "Being and non-being rise together" in Ch. 2.

CHAPTER 41

1   *When the highest type of man¹ hears Tao,*
2   *He practices it diligently.*
3   *When the middle type hears Tao,*
4   *He half believes and half disbelieves it.*
5   *When the lowest type hears Tao,*
6   *He laughs out loud.*
7   *If he didn't,*
8   *It couldn't possibly be considered Tao.*
9   *Therefore the* Chien yen *has it:*
10   *"The bright Tao looks dark;*
11   *The forward-moving Tao seems retreating;*
12   *The level Tao seems bumpy;*
13   *The highest Te is like a valley;*
14   *Perfect white looks soiled;*
15   *The broad Te seems insufficient;*
16   *The firm Te seems precarious;*
17   *The pure Te² seems discolored;*
18   *The great square has no corners;*
19   *The great vessel takes long to complete;*
20   *The great sound is inaudible;*
21   *The great form is shapeless."*
22   *Tao is hidden and nameless.*
23   *Truly, Tao alone supports [all things] and brings them to completion.*

The "middle type" is skeptical when he is told of Tao, because he is unsure of what is invisible. He still lacks transcendental vision; Tao is thus "hidden" from his view. When told of Tao, the "lowest type" laughs out loud because he simply dismisses whatever is not visible. Now, "if he [upon hearing Tao] didn't laugh," it would mean that he had misidentified it as something visible or finite.

Chien yen was probably the title of an ancient text.[3] The twelve lines attributed to it (10-21), however, do sound much like Lao Tzu's own words, not only in sense but also in style. Notice the poetry of the passage.[4] Any literal or analytic reading would be out of place. All of these paradoxical lines are intended to convey one single message: go beyond the visible, beyond names. For "Tao is hidden and nameless."

Notes

[1] I have translated *shih* as "man." The rendering of the character as "scholar/official" in the Confucian sense is inappropriate here. Etymologically—that is, originally—*shih* does mean "male" as opposed to "female." According to Tōdō Akiyasu, it is a pictograph expressive of the penis. See Tōdō, pp. 127-128.

[2] Read *te* for *chen*. See Fukunaga, Vol. 2, p. 37.

[3] But it could have meant simply "proverb." See Fukunaga, Vol. 2, p. 35.

[4] The poetry of the lines is evident in the original text, where the twelve four-character lines are all in rhyme. See Fukunaga, Vol. 2, p. 35.

CHAPTER 42

1   *Tao gives birth to One;*
2   *One gives birth to Two;*
3   *Two give birth to Three,*
4   *Three give birth to the ten thousand things.*
5   *The ten thousand things carry the yin on their backs and hold the yang in their arms;*
6   *And attain harmony through the blending of the two energies.*
7   *What people detest most*
8   *Is to be orphaned, widowed and ill-provided.*
9   *But that is how kings and princes call themselves.*
10 *Therefore, of things, some gain by losing,*
11 *Some lose by gaining.*
12 *What others teach*
13 *I also teach.*
14 *"The violent one will not attain his death."*
15 *I will take this to be my teacher.*

The first four lines are commonly interpreted to state Lao Tzu's cosmology: the cosmic lineage from Tao to the birth of the ten thousand things. According to this traditional reading, "One" is identified as "being" (*yu*), "Two" as "*yin* and *yang*," and "Three" (rather awkwardly) as the product of the union of these two forces.[1] I suppose such an interpretation is certainly possible but not necessary. What we find in these lines is a numerical representation of the process by which the ten thousand things come into existence. But such a schematic formulation can hardly give any meaningful, concrete picture of the coming into being of the cosmos.[2] (The numbers in the formula are empirically undefined.)

A word about Lao Tzu's cosmology. If he had a definite cosmology, it would seem hardly to have differed from the traditional one, except in one important respect. As I pointed out in my comment on Chapter 1, he only took the old cosmology one step further, by claiming that Heaven and Earth, too, came from Tao, the ultimate source. At the same time, he, too, believed that Heaven and Earth were the life-givers and nurturers of the ten thousand things.[3]

With lines 10-11, Lao Tzu returns to the subject of humanity's desire for gain and aversion to loss. In a universe, where you "gain by losing" and "lose by gaining," what would gain and loss really mean?

To "attain one's death" is to fulfill one's Tao-given life, that is, to die a natural death. The violent man fails to "attain his death." Violence is violence to life, hence contrary to Tao.

Notes

[1] See Fukunaga, Vol. 2, pp. 39-41; Morohashi, p. 91.

[2] Though it may be taken to mean the universal multiplication of beings through Tao's generative force.

[3] This belief is evident in various passages: e.g., Chs. 16, 23, 25, 32. In Ch. 25, one reads the following lines: "The measure for man is Earth;/ The measure for Earth is Heaven;/ The measure for Heaven is Tao." This passage clearly reflects the ancient Chinese cosmology, which believed in the hierarchy of "Heaven-Earth-Man." Of course, Lao Tzu goes one step further.

CHAPTER 43

1　*The softest under Heaven*
2　*Rides roughshod over the hardest under Heaven.*
3　*The beingless [wu yu] penetrates the spaceless [wu chien].*[1]
4　*From this I know the advantage of no-action [wu-wei].*
5　*The wordless teaching,*
6　*The advantage of no-action—*
7　*Nothing under Heaven exemplifies them better.*

In the opening two lines, Lao Tzu refers to water by the "softest under Heaven," and rock by the "hardest under Heaven." Thus, he once again affirms the "soft" and "weak" prevailing over the "hard" and "strong." One may detect the double meaning of line 3. At the immediate level, it states the capacity of the "softest" to "penetrate" the "hardest," while, at another, deeper level, it points to the capacity of Tao ("what is not") to "penetrate" all beings ("what is").

Water exemplifies the "advantage of no-action," which is its "wordless teaching." Note the identity of "no-action" and "wordless teaching."[2]

Notes

[1]　I translate *wu yu* in this line as "beingless" rather than "non-being" in order to indicate the repeated use of the negative particle *wu* in *wu yu* ("no being") and *wu chien* ("no space"). Notice the occurrence of *wu* once again in the next line.

[2]　Recall the following lines from Ch. 2: "Therefore, the sage/ Relies on no-action,/ Practices wordless teaching."

104

CHAPTER 44

1 *Your name or your body, which is dearer?*
2 *Your body or your possessions, which is more valuable?*
3 *Gaining or losing, which worries you more?*
4 *Therefore, when your craving is excessive, your spending is extravagant.*
5 *When you store much, you are bound to lose much.*
6 *Know how to be content, and you will not be disgraced.*
7 *Know when to stop, and you will be free from danger.*
8 *Thus you will be long-lasting.*

In the first three lines, Lao Tzu once again reminds us of the importance of the care of one's own body above everything else. People, however, neglect to take care of the only thing that is truly precious, in pursuit of good names and possessions. In line 3, "gaining" means gaining "name" or "possessions," while "losing" means losing one's own "body."

The message of the rest of the chapter is clear. "Know how to be content."

CHAPTER 45

1   *Great accomplishment looks incomplete;*
2   *Use will not wear it out.*
3   *Great fullness looks empty;*
4   *Use will not exhaust it.*
5   *Great straightness looks crooked;*
6   *Great skill looks clumsy;*
7   *Great eloquence sounds stuttering;*
8   *"Being in motion overcomes cold;*
9   *Being still overcomes heat."*
10   *Be clear and still, and you will be the lord of all under Heaven.*

I read this chapter in three parts.[1] In the first part (lines 1-4) Lao Tzu describes once again the working of Tao. "Tao never does [*wu wei*],/ Yet leaves nothing undone" (Ch. 37). Its "accomplishment" is great yet seems "incomplete" in the human eyes. It is "empty, yet inexhaustible"—as if it were a cosmic bellows. "Ever active, it gives off more and more" (Ch. 5). Its "fullness" is indeed its "emptiness."

Lines 5-7 do follow the paradoxical logic of lines 1 and 3. I read them, however, as statements intended to subvert the common values of "straightness" (*chih*), "skill" (*ch'iao*), and "eloquence" (*pien*). Here Lao Tzu is not affirming the virtues of "crookedness," "clumsiness," and "stuttering"; rather, he is rejecting the very opposition of "straightness"/"crookedness," "skill"/ "clumsiness," and "eloquence"/"stuttering."

I read lines 8-9 as a proverb. The last line evokes once again the "still" (*ching*) image of the sage, who does nothing. Its connection with the proverb seems tenuous, though the word "still" occurs also in line 9.

Notes

[1] Fukunaga notes two different rhyme patterns in lines 1-4 and lines 5-7. The last three lines are not in rhyme. See Fukunaga, Vol. 2, pp. 53-54.

CHAPTER 46

1   *When Tao prevails under Heaven,*
2   *Fleet-footed horses are taken out [of service] to fertilize the*
     fields.
3   *When Tao fails to prevail under Heaven,*
4   *War horses breed on the sacred mounds outside the city*
     walls.[1]
5   *No misfortune is greater than not knowing contentment;*
6   *No calamity is greater than wanting to possess.*
7   *Therefore, he who knows the sufficiency of contentment*
8   *Is always contented.*

In time of peace "fleet-footed horses" are no longer needed in battlefields; therefore, they are used "to fertilize the fields." In time of war "war horses" camp everywhere, so they "breed on the sacred mounts." War comes when "Tao fails to prevail under Heaven."[2]—that is, when people fail to follow Tao.

In the remainder, Lao Tzu returns to the subject of contentment. Note that contentment for him means "desirelessness," especially freedom from all man-made desires.

Notes

[1]   I follow Waley's translation of *chiao*. See Waley, p. 199, and also p. 254 ("Additional Notes").

[2]   This phrase (*t'ien hsia wu tao*) is a set phrase, which refers to a time of political or social upheavals.

CHAPTER 47

1   *Without leaving the door,*
2   *You may know all under Heaven.*
3   *Without looking out the window,*
4   *You may know the way of Heaven.*
5   *The further you go,*
6   *The less you know.*
7   *Therefore the sage*
8   *Knows without going,*
9   *Sees without looking,*
10 *Fulfills without doing.*

The sage "knows all under Heaven [*t'ien tao*]," namely, Tao. His knowing is no-knowing and his seeing is no-seeing, just as his doing is no-doing (*wu wei*). You don't "leave the door" or "look out the window" to see what is invisible.

Perhaps, lines 1 and 3 may suggest a picture of the sage meditating in a dark room shut off from the outside world. Nothing could be farther from the truth. The sage is indeed the man of "emptiness" and "stillness." But he is at the same time a man of nature. Nature is his home. Why would he seek such an arbitrary seclusion? "The great Tao overflows left and right" (Ch. 34), like a cosmic deluge. He finds Tao everywhere.

Lines 5-6 tell us: The more you learn human things, the farther you go away from Tao. (This is exactly what the opening lines of the next chapter state.) Keep in mind that in ancient China learners were goers, who had to travel all over the Middle Kingdom in search of teachers of great reputation. But to learn what?

CHAPTER 48

1   *When you pursue learning, you gain day by day.*
2   *When you pursue Tao, you lose day by day.*
3   *You lose more and more,*
4   *Until you reach thereby the point of no-action.*
5   *You do nothing yet leave nothing undone.*
6   *You take all under Heaven*
7   *Always through no activity.*
8   *Should you rely on activity,*
9   *You will find it insufficient to take all under Heaven.*

Learning was considered to be an additive process in ancient China,[1] as it is in today's information age. "When you pursue learning," you accumulate more and more in your head. On the other hand, "when you pursue Tao," you rid yourself of whatever you have acquired, until you reach the state of emptiness, which is the state of selflessness.

Being selfless, "you do nothing [*wu wei*] yet leave nothing undone." Does this sentence sound odd? Wouldn't it rather be that when you do nothing, you would leave nothing done, rather than undone? Note that the man of *wu-wei* intends nothing to be "done," *therefore,* he *finds* "nothing undone." It is only by the logic of intention that one *finds* something "undone." Only those who intend something to be done find something undone.

Notes

[1]   Here Lao Tzu is rejecting Confucius's emphasis on learning. See Appendix I.

CHAPTER 49

1 *The sage has no fixed mind;*
2 *He takes the people's mind as his own.*
3 *I accept as good those who are good;*
4 *I also accept as good those who are not good.*
5 *Such is Te's goodness.*
6 *I trust those who trust;*
7 *I also trust those who do not trust.*
8 *Such is Te's trust.*
9 *The sage, in ruling all under Heaven,*
10 *Makes his mind one with it.*
11 *All his subjects set their ears and eyes on him.*
12 *He regards them all as his children.*

The sage is selfless. That is to say, he has no set idea or belief about anything. What does Lao Tzu mean by the "people's mind"? Doesn't the sage "make [the people's] minds empty"? Yes. This does not mean that he turns them into insentient or unfeeling beings, like trees or rocks. The second line asserts the sage's selfless identity with the people's joys and pains. Lao Tzu reiterates the same point later in lines 9-10.

In the next six lines (3-8), Lao Tzu speaks of the sage's indiscriminate acceptance of all his subjects: bad ones as well as good ones, untrusting ones as well as trusting ones. He makes no distinction between "those who are good" and "those who are not good," and between "those who trust" and "those who do not trust." Such is the sage's "goodness" and "trust"; he is all-embracing, like nature itself.

The last two lines may sound paternalistic. But keep in mind that the relationship between the sage and his people is neither one of power nor one in which one gives and the other receives orders. The sage rules through no-action. It is because of his "mysterious Te" that "All his subjects set their ears and eyes on him." Not that he directs his people by word or by some sort of sign. His leadership is wordless. Recall the following line: "Of the rulers, the best is one of whose existence the people are [merely] aware" (Ch. 17).

CHAPTER 50

1   *You come out to life and enter death.*
2   *The companions of life are three in ten;*[1]
3   *The companions of death are three in ten:*
4   *The way humans live,*
5   *There are those who move into death-spots.*
6   *They too are three in ten.*
7   *Why is this so?*
8   *It is because of their hoarding of life.*
9   *I hear that those who nurture life well,*
10   *When traveling on land, do not meet wild buffaloes or tigers,*
11   *Nor do they, when going into battle, put on armor or shields.*
12   *The wild buffalo would find no place to thrust its horns;*
13   *The tiger would find no place to place its claws;*
14   *The sword would find no place to lodge its blade.*
15   *Why is this so?*
16   *Because for such men there are no death-spots.*

In the first part (lines 1-6), Lao Tzu speaks of three types of people: "companions of life," "companions of death," and "those who move into death-spots." The first type are those who follow the way of life, Tao, and the second are those who follow the way of death, the way contrary to Tao. But what does he mean by the third type?

The word "death-spot" (*shih ti*)[2] is a military term, meaning a position of great danger. What sort of people are "those who move into death-spots"? It is to be noted that these are not reckless people, who have no regard for life at all. On the contrary, they are those who seek to preserve their life with their conscious effort. They are those who "hoard life," relying on their own wits and acts (*wei*). Thus, they have lost their oneness with Tao's life-world. It is this loss of oneness with life—their attachment to their separate selves—that brings about their vulnerability, their "death-spots." By contrast, "those who nurture life well" simply live (and die) following Tao—as all creatures in nature do—and never seek a life separate from the whole. It is their oneness with Tao's life-world that makes them invulnerable. Like "newborn babies," they have no "death-spots."[3]

There now follows Lao Tzu's fantastic story of the invulnerability of the true nurturer of life, who can be hurt neither by a wild beast nor by the sword.[4] The reader may be inclined to ask: Did Lao Tzu *really* believe in such a story? The question is beside the point. For what we have here is a *story* intended to illustrate the invulnerability of "those who nurture life well," in contrast to the vulnerability of those who "hoard life." Freedom from "death-spots" means at the same time freedom from "life-spots," inasmuch as subjection to "death-spots" comes from the creation of "life-spots." For "those who nurture life well" there exist neither "death-spots" nor "life-spots"—indeed, neither life nor death. They live in the nameless.

Notes

[1]   There are two ways of reading *shih yu san*: either as "thirteen" or as "three in ten." The latter seems more appropriate.

[2]   I follow Waley's translation of *szu ti*. See Waley, p. 203.

[3]   See Ch. 55.

[4]   A similar passage appears in the *Chuang Tzu*. The Lord of the Yellow River asks Jo of the North Sea: "Why is Tao to be honored?" In the middle of his reply, the latter says: "When a man has perfect Te, fire cannot burn him, water cannot drown him, cold and heat cannot afflict him, birds and beasts cannot injure him." *Chuang Tzu*, Ch. 17. See Watson, p. 182.

CHAPTER 51

1   *Tao gives life [to the ten thousand things];*
2   *Te nurtures them.*
3   *Materiality shapes them;*[1]
4   *The circumstances fulfill them.*
5   *Therefore, of the ten thousand things*
6   *None fails to revere Tao and honor Te.*
7   *The revering of Tao,*
8   *The honoring of Te—*
9   *No one orders it.*
10   *It is always so of itself [tzu-jan].*
11   *Therefore Tao gives them life;*
12   *Te nurtures them.*
13   *Makes them flourish and grow;*
14   *Gives them security and comfort;*
15   *Feeds and shelters them.*
16   *To give them life, without possessing them;*
17   *To rule them, without depending on them;*
18   *To lead them, without presiding over them—*
19   *This is called the mysterious Te.*

Lao Tzu sings once again of the life-giving, life-sustaining Tao. The first two lines and the last four have appeared in Chapter 10.[2]

The ten thousand things "revere Tao and honor Te," simply by "being so of themselves" (*tzu-jan*)—that is, by fulfilling their Tao-given nature. So the people, too, "revere" the sage by "being so of themselves." Recall the closing lines of Chapter 17: "Yet the task is accomplished;/ The people call me *tzu-jan*."

Notes

[1] The meaning of this line is uncertain, and my translation tentative.
[2] The original text has no grammatical subject when the first two lines appear in Ch. 10.

CHAPTER 52

1   *All under Heaven has its beginning,*
2   *Which may be regarded as the mother of all under Heaven.*
3   *Having recognized its mother,*
4   *You know the child, also;*
5   *Having known the child,*
6   *You hold fast to its mother, also.*
7   *Thus you will be free of danger till the end of your life.*
8   *Block the holes,*
9   *Shut the gates,*
10 *And you will never be spent till your last day.*
11 *Open up the holes,*
12 *Busy yourself with activities,*
13 *And you will never be saved till your last day.*
14 *To see what is small is called clear sight;*
15 *To hold fast to what is soft is called strength.*
16 *Use the light,*
17 *Return to clear sight,*
18 *And you will never bring misfortune upon yourself.*
19 *This is called following the constant.*

In the opening two lines, Lao Tzu announces "the mother of all under Heaven," namely, Tao. But how many recognize the "mother"? She is "invisible" and "inaudible."

Lines 3-7 may be read especially in view of the fact that the multitude fails to recognize "the mother of all under Heaven." You do not "know the child" until you "recognize its mother." Now that you recognize the mother, "you know [her] child, also." Knowing the child, "hold fast to its mother, also."

In the middle part (8-13), the "holes" and "gates" broadly

refer to the human faculties that come in contact with the external world.[1] Close off your faculties to all temptations of civilization, such as the "five colors," the "five tones," and "rare goods." Does this mean that you should block all your outer senses? No. To do so would be contrary to human nature as a sentient being.

Turning to the last part, notice the parallelism between lines 14-15. Humanity exalts what is great and what is hard (strong), and despises what is small and what is soft (weak). Only a man of "clear sight" sees the greatness of what is small and the strength of what is soft. "Return to clear sight"; "follow the constant [Tao]."

Notes

[1] The "holes" are commonly interpreted to refer to the sense organs, while the "gates" are variously understood to mean either "desire," "cunning," "mind," or "intelligence." See Fukunaga, Vol. 2, p. 85; Morohashi, p. 106; Chan (1963b), p. 192; Lau, p. 113.

CHAPTER 53

1   *Let me have even the slightest of wisdom.*
2   *Traveling the great way [Tao],*
3   *I will only fear going astray.*
4   *The great way is level.*
5   *Yet people prefer small paths.*
6   *The court is overrun with corruption;*
7   *The fields are overgrown with weeds;*
8   *The granaries are utterly empty;*
9   *Yet the officials wear embroidered clothes,*
10   *Carry sharp swords,*
11   *Feast on food and wine,*
12   *Possess more goods than they need.*
13   *This is called the robber's extravagance.*
14   *It is indeed contrary to Tao!*

In the first part (lines 1-5), Lao Tzu speaks of the peace of mind of one who follows Tao. Notice the contrast between the "great way" (Tao) and "small paths" (*ching*). Tao is "level" and easy to follow; yet, people choose treacherous, "small paths."

In the remainder of the chapter, one reads Lao Tzu's sharpest critique of the ruling classes. In his eyes, the rulers are "robbers"; they are distinguishable from common burglars only by the scale of their thievery.[1]

Notes

[1]   The same view is also expressed in Chuang Tzu's story of Robber Chih, in which he accuses the (Confucian) sages of aiding rulers in their global robbery, their plundering of the state. See *Chunag Tzu*, Ch. 10; Watson, p. 110.

CHAPTER 54

1   *What is firmly planted cannot be pulled out;*
2   *What is tightly held in the arms cannot slip away,*
3   *So that the descendants will never stop offering ancestral*
        sacrifice.
4   *Cultivate it in yourself,*
5   *And its Te will be genuine.*
6   *Cultivate it in the household,*
7   *And its Te will be more than sufficient.*
8   *Cultivate it in the village,*
9   *And its Te will be long-lasting.*
10   *Cultivate it in the state,*
11   *And its Te will be plentiful.*
12   *Cultivate it in all under Heaven,*
13   *And its Te will be all-encompassing.*
14   *Therefore, observe yourself through yourself;*[1]
15   *The household through the household;*
16   *The village through the village;*
17   *The state through the state;*
18   *All under Heaven through all under Heaven.*
19   *How do I know that all under Heaven is so?*
20   *With this.*

This chapter could have easily appeared in a Confucian text.[2] I read it as a futile attempt to appropriate Lao Tzu within Confucian tradition.[3]

    The first three lines are commonly interpreted to mean: If you live the life of Tao, holding fast to Tao and never letting it go, your offspring will never fail to offer you the rite of ancestral sacrifice. The passage so interpreted seems intended to offer a Confucian incentive for the life of Tao. According to Lao Tzu, however, the life of Tao is that of the "uncarved block" (*p'u*), free of all human conventions. How is it possible that one who has returned to the "uncarved block" would be concerned with such things as the rite (*li*) of ancestral sacrifice?

Presumably, what is to be "cultivated" in one's "person," the "household," etc., in lines 4-13, is Tao. Yes, with the cultivation of Tao, one's Te will be "genuine," "long-lasting," etc. However, one may detect in these lines a certain hollowness, which comes from the abstractness of the passage. The meaning of the last seven lines is uncertain—if they mean anything at all.

Notes

[1] I am giving a literal translation of this and the next four lines; their meaning is uncertain.

[2] Line 3 refers to "ancestral sacrifice," one of the most important Confucian rites. Furthermore, the widening circle of "cultivation" mentioned follows exactly the Confucian prescription for the ascending order of the levels of mastery, beginning with "self-cultivation" (*hsiu shen*) to the "regulating of the household" (*ch'i chia*), to the "ordering of the state" (*chih kuo*), and culminating with "bringing peace to all under Heaven" (*p'ing t'ien hsia*). Even the language and logic of the chapter sound more like those of the Confucian texts than those of Lao Tzu. Compare the following passage from The *Great Learning* (*Ta Hsüeh*):

> The ancients who wished to manifest their bright Te to all under Heaven first brought order to their states. Those who wished to bring order to their states first regulated their households. Those who wished to regulate their households first cultivated their persons . . . .

[3] I say "futile" because Lao Tzu's teachings are fundamentally antithetical to Confucius's. For example, Tao is *nature's* way for the former, but the *human* way for the latter. See Appendix I.

CHAPTER 55

1   *He who possesses Te in abundance*
2   *May be likened to a newborn baby.*
3   *Bees, scorpions and vipers do not sting it;*
4   *Ferocious beasts do not seize it;*
5   *Birds of prey do not attack it.*
6   *Its bones are weak and its sinews soft, yet its grip is firm.*
7   *It doesn't yet know the union of male and female, yet its organ is erect.*
8   *Its vital energy is perfect.*
9   *It screams all day yet never becomes hoarse.*
10 *Its harmony is perfect.*
11 *To know harmony is called [to know the] constant.*
12 *To know the constant is called enlightenment.*
13 *To improve upon one's life is called ill omen.*
14 *When the mind dictates the vital breath, it is called forcing.*
15 *When a thing reaches its prime, it becomes old.*
16 *Forcing is called contrary to Tao.*
17 *What is contrary to Tao expires early.*

Te is Tao's power. It is vital force, inasmuch as Tao is the very principle of life. Therefore, "He who possesses Te in abundance/ May be likened to a newborn baby." Such a man has returned to the state of infancy. In lines 3-10, Lao Tzu describes the visible manifestation of Te in the being of a "newborn baby," the true carrier of Te. What is particularly revealing here is his reference to the vital urge in the baby: its budding potency. I take this to be indicative of Lao Tzu's vitalistic (or biological) conception of Tao and of Te.

Line 10 refers to the baby's "perfect" "harmony" (*ho*). Harmony with what? Harmony with its own nature, that is, with Tao. *Ho* here means agreement with, or being attuned to, nature. The newborn baby "screams all day yet never becomes hoarse," because its screaming is perfectly *at one with* (its) nature. There is no forcing against its Tao-given capacity.

"To know harmony [*ho*]" is "to know the constant [*ch'ang*]." Be attuned to the eternal Tao. Note that "knowing" (*chih*) here means the "enlightened" state of awareness, not intellectual knowledge.[1]

By "improving upon life" (*i sheng*) Lao Tzu means living beyond one's Tao-appointed life. To do so would be to go against Tao. Therefore, it is an "ill omen." Lao Tzu here attributes man's attempt to "improve upon his life" to the human mind's "dictating the vital breath." He calls it "forcing," since it is the mind's act (*wei*) against Tao—something one observes only among humans and no other living things. (In the newborn infant there is no "mind dictating the vital breath"; hence, "its harmony is perfect.") The last three lines have appeared in Chapter 30.

Notes

[1] See Appendix II.

CHAPTER 56

1   *He who knows does not speak;*
2   *He who speaks does not know.*
3   *Block the holes,*
4   *Shut the gates.*
5   *[He]¹ blunts the sharpness,*
6   *Unravels the tangles,*
7   *Softens the brilliance,*
8   *Identifies with the dust.*
9   *This is called mysterious identity.*
10 *Therefore you can neither befriend him,²*
11 *Nor alienate him,*
12 *Nor benefit him,*
13 *Nor harm him,*
14 *Nor exalt him,*
15 *Nor humble him.*
16 *That is why he is the noblest of all under Heaven.*

"He who knows does not speak." What does he "know"? The "nameless." The "nameless" cannot be "spoken" of "He who speaks does not know." What does he "not know"? Of course, the nameless. What he "speaks" of is necessarily something "named" or "nameable."

The next six lines have already appeared: lines 3-4 in Chapter 52 and lines 5-8 in Chapter 4. I have commented on the first two in their previous occurrence. The sage "blunts" all human wits, "unravels" all man-made entanglements, "softens" all brilliance of civilization, and "identifies" with the lowliest.³ This "identity with the dust" is "mysterious," for no one can attain it as long as he lives in the name-mediated, human universe of values.⁴

In the remaining lines (10-16), Lao Tzu describes the absolute nature of the sage. Like Tao itself, he is *above* all human relationships, such as "befriending," "alienating," "benefiting," etc. That is why he is a "holy man," the noblest of all creatures.[5]

Notes

[1]   The text has no subject in this and the next three lines. I provide "he" (the sage) as the subject here. In the previous appearance of the same lines in Ch. 4, however, I provided "it" (Tao) as the subject in view of the context of the chapter.

[2]   The text has no grammatical object in this and the remaining lines.

[3]   I am commenting on these lines (5-8) here, rather than in their previous appearance in Ch. 4, primarily for rhetorical reasons. In the original text each line consists of three characters, with the identical *ch'i* in the middle. Lines 3-8, forming three pairs (3 and 4; 5 and 6; 7 and 8), are in rhyme. See Fukunaga, Vol. 2, p. 107.

[4]   See my comment on Ch. 28.

[5]   Recall that *sheng jen* ("sage") literally means "holy man."

CHAPTER 57

1   *"Govern the state according to what is right;*
2   *Use the troops by surprise tactics."*
3   *But take all under Heaven through no-action.*
4   *How do I know this is so?*
5   *Because of this—*
6   *The more bans and taboos under Heaven,*
7   *The poorer the people;*
8   *The more sharp instruments in the hands of the people,*
9   *The more trouble for the state;*
10 *The more skills the people have,*
11 *The more fanciful inventions appear;*
12 *The more laws and decrees,*
13 *The more thieves and robbers.*
14 *Therefore the sage says:*
15 *"I engage in no-action, and the people transform of themselves;*
16 *I love stillness, and the people correct themselves;*
17 *I engage in no work, and the people prosper of themselves;*
18 *I am free from desire, and the people turn into the uncarved block of themselves."*

The opening two lines might have been a common saying of the time.[1] Line 3, however, implies that neither "rightness" (*cheng*) nor "surprise tactic" (*ch'i*) is the way to "take all under Heaven." In lines 6-13, we read Lao Tzu's sweeping critique of social and legal institutions as well as of weaponry and technology—all key elements of human civilization. "Bans and taboos" make the people poorer; "sharp instruments" make society violent; "skills" beget monstrosities; and "laws and decrees" turn men into criminals.

The last four lines sum up neatly what has been said of the sage in many scattered passages.

Notes

[1]   See Fukunaga, Vol. 2, p. 110.

CHAPTER 58

1   *When the government is dull,*
2   *The people are simple.*
3   *When the government is keen,*
4   *The people are discontented.*
5   *Bad fortune is what good fortune leans on;*
6   *Good fortune is where bad fortune lurks.*
7   *Who knows the fortune's end?*
8   *There is nothing straight.*
9   *What is straight turns monstrous.*
10 *What is beautiful turns grotesque.*
11 *Man has been deluded*
12 *From time immemorial.*
13 *Therefore the sage*
14 *Is square without cutting;*
15 *Honest without scraping;*
16 *Straight without overbearing;*
17 *Bright without dazzling.*

"Dull" is the sage's rule. He does nothing (*wu wei*); therefore the people are "simple" and contented. When the government is "keen," on the other hand, it is constantly in action (*wei*), dictating and forcing; therefore, the people are "discontented."

In the middle eight lines (5-12), Lao Tzu is pointing to man's propensity to view whatever happens to him in terms of "good" or "bad" fortune. "Good" fortune and "bad" fortune only reflect man's wishes and desires. "Who knows the fortune's end?" In fact, nothing ends, and therefore nothing *is* "good" or "bad." It is only our name-bound perspective that sees the beginning and end of things. "Good" fortune and "bad" fortune succeed one another.

The last five lines may be read as a song of the mystery of the sage's rule.

CHAPTER 59

1 *In ruling the people and serving Heaven*
2 *Nothing is better than being sparing.*
3 *Truly, being sparing*
4 *Means submitting early.*
5 *Submitting early*
6 *Means accumulating Te heavily.*
7 *If you accumulate Te heavily,*
8 *There will be nothing you cannot overcome.*
9 *If there is nothing you cannot overcome,*
10 *You will find no limit.*
11 *If you find no limit,*
12 *You will be fit to rule a state.*
13 *If you possess the mother of the state,*
14 *You will be long-lasting.*
15 *This is called deeply rooted and firmly planted.*
16 *It is the way of long life and lasting sight.*

In the first two lines, Lao Tzu declares that "being sparing" (*se*) is the best way of "ruling the people and serving Heaven." What a puzzling statement! What does he mean by "being sparing"? The next two lines are no less baffling. "Submitting early" to what? I think the key to the understanding of these and subsequent lines lies in keeping in mind the basic meaning of *se*.

The character *se* etymologically means the unwillingness of a farmer to part with his wheat that has been stored away in his granary. Its basic meaning is thus unwillingness to spend, or, rather, the absence of the desire to spend. For this reason, the character has the derivative meaning of "miserliness." It must be stressed, however, that *se* does not necessarily imply covetousness, which we tend to associate with "miserliness." Indeed, in this chapter, it means the absence of covetousness. In view of this basic meaning of *se*, we may interpret the two opening lines to mean: the best way of "ruling the people and serving Heaven" is to be free of covetousness, like a good "sparing" farmer. Notice that the image of "sparing" farmer represents the very counter-image of covetous man, the product of civilization.[1] The farmer is a man of least desires or simple desires, devoid of all man-made desires and values, like the sage himself.

Once we understand Lao Tzu's meaning of *se* in this way, it may not be too difficult to understand lines 3-4. The "sparing" farmer is one who lives closest to nature—that is, to Tao—unspoiled by the vanity of civilization. "Truly, being sparing/ Means submitting early." "Submitting" (*fu*) here means "submitting" to Tao. Why does Lao Tzu add "early" (*tsao*)? I interpret him to suggest the "submission" of the "sparing" farmer to Tao from the start. Of all the rulers, only the sage "submits [to Tao] early," like the "sparing" farmer. Thanks to his "early submission," he "accumulates Te heavily." He is "fit to rule a state."

By the "mother of the state" Lao Tzu means Tao. Who "possesses" her? One who follows her. Such a one is "deeply rooted and firmly planted"; therefore, he is "long-lasting."[2]

Notes

[1] It may be interesting to note that a farmer in ancient times was sometimes called *se fu* (literally, "miserly man"). Perhaps the negative connotation of *se* or "miserliness" may simply reflect the negative attitude of the "civilized" man toward those who are unwilling to "spend" except for life's necessities.

[2] The closing line is often cited by the followers of Taoist religion as a statement of "immortal" life. See Fukunaga, Vol. 2, p. 120.

Chapter 60

1   *Governing a large state*
2   *Is like boiling a small fish.*
3   *When you rule all under Heaven according to Tao,*
4   *The spirits of the dead cease to exercise supernatural power.*
5   *It is not that they cease to exercise supernatural power.*
6   *Their supernatural power does not harm the people.*
7   *It is not simply that their supernatural power does not harm the people.*
8   *The sage, too, does not harm the people.*
9   *Since neither of them harms the people,*
10   *Their Te, united, returns.*

A good cook handles a delicate fish as little as possible for fear that he should ruin it. Similarly, a good ruler meddles with the people's affairs as little as possible. The sage does not meddle with them at all.

All powers (Te), natural or supernatural, derive from Tao. Therefore, they, "united, return" to benefit the people when the ruler governs according to Tao. Even the "spirits of the dead," feared by the living, would cease to "harm the people." Line 8 may strike the reader as strange. How would it be possible that the sage should "harm the people"? But we have read in Chapter 5: "The sage treats the people as straw dogs." Expressed in these lines is Lao Tzu's concern for the simple wellbeing of the people: how to keep them safe from being harmed by all agents of power.

CHAPTER 61

1   *The large state is the lower reaches of a river,*
2   *The place where all under Heaven meets—*
3   *The female of all under Heaven.*
4   *The female always overcomes the male by stillness.*
5   *With stillness she plays the lower part.*
6   *Therefore, when the large state plays the lower part toward the small state,*
7   *It takes the small state.*
8   *When the small state plays the lower part toward the large state,*
9   *It takes the large state.*
10   *Therefore some take by playing the lower part;*
11   *Some are taken by playing the lower part.*
12   *The large state merely wants to unite with the other and nurture it;*
13   *The small state merely wants to join and serve the other.*
14   *Each gets what it wants.*
15   *It is right that the large state should play the lower part.*

Picture the large state as Lao Tzu describes in its relation to the small state. How radically different it is from the way a large state in reality generally acts vis-à-vis a small one! Consider his image of the large state as the "female of all under Heaven" especially in view of his time. That was the Warring States period, when all major powers were constantly engaged in warfare, as they were contending for supremacy, conquering and absorbing smaller, weaker states. The image one could have of these large states would be rather the exact opposite of Lao Tzu's large state that "plays the lower part toward the small state." What he is presenting here is nothing less than his vision of the proper role of the large state as the "female [rather than the "male"] of all under Heaven."

Lines 4-5 suggest that the large state should conduct itself toward the small state with "stillness," that is, never demanding or forcing. It should act through no-action (*wu wei*).

The middle lines (6-11) are most interesting. Here Lao Tzu presents *both* the large state and the small state as "playing the lower part." Here we have a picture of the world in which all states, large and small, act according to the female principles of non-contention and passivity in their mutual dealings.

In lines 12-13 Lao Tzi states how such a world would serve well both the large and the small state in terms of what each seeks. "The large state merely wants to unite with the other and nurture it;/ The small state merely want to join and serve the other." Evident in these lines is Lao Tzu's vision of the harmonious relationship between states based on the common enterprise dedicated to the principle of life. What a dream for him to have, considering the reality in which he lived! On the other hand, it was perhaps that reality that made him dream of such a world.

CHAPTER 62

1   *Tao*
2   *Is the sanctuary of the ten thousand things,*
3   *The good man's treasure,*
4   *The bad man's refuge.*
5   *Beautiful words can buy honor,*
6   *Beautiful deeds can benefit people.*
7   *Though a man may be bad,*
8   *How can he be abandoned?*
9   *Therefore, on occasion of crowning the Son of Heaven*
10   *Or installing the three ministers of state,*
11   *Rather than present a large disc of jade, accompanied by a team of four horses,*
12   *Better remain in your seat and offer a tribute of this Tao.*
13   *Why did the ancients honor this Tao?*
14   *Did they not say: "You get thereby what you seek;*
15   *You escape thereby when you have sinned."*
16   *Therefore they regarded it as the most precious of all things under Heaven.*

How can Tao be both the "good man's treasure" and the "bad man's refuge"? Because it is the very principle of life, the "sanctuary of the ten thousand things." Nothing can live apart from it. It is life's way. Both the "good man" and the "bad man" live by the same Tao. But the good man sees it as his "treasure," because he "gets thereby what [he] seeks," whereas the bad man sees it as his "refuge," because he "escapes thereby when [he] has sinned." The "good man" speaks "beautiful words," thus gaining "honor" from his fellows, and performs "beautiful deeds," "benefiting people." The "bad man" does neither. But Tao does not "abandon" him.

Indeed, "good" and "bad" exist only in man's name-bound universe, and not under the aspect of Tao.

A "large disc of jade" and a "team of four horses" are of great value in the human world; so they are offered as presents to the "Son of Heaven" and the "three ministers of state." But such things are valuable in name only; they have nothing to do with life. Do you want to make a present of the "most precious of all things under Heaven"? Then present Tao.

CHAPTER 63

1   *Act through no-action,*
2   *Attend to no-affair,*
3   *Relish no-flavor,*
4   *Take the small as big and the few as many.*
5   *Repay hatred with Te.*
6   *Plan difficult things while they are easy.*
7   *Handle big things while they are small.*
8   *Difficult things under Heaven*
9   *Always arise from what is easy;*
10   *Big things under Heaven*
11   *Always arise from what is small.*
12   *For this reason the sage*
13   *Never intends big things,*
14   *And thus can accomplish big things.*
15   *He who agrees lightly invariably inspires little faith.*
16   *He who considers many things easy invariably encounters many difficulties.*
17   *For this reason even the sage considers things difficult;*
18   *Therefore he never encounters difficulties.*

In the first three lines Lao Tzu again calls for return to nature: to the life of "no-action" (*wu-wei*), "no-affair" (*wu shih*) and "no-flavor" (*wu wei*).

Line 5 may be read especially in view of the following exchange between Confucius and his interlocutor. In one of his sayings, Confucius is asked: "What about the saying 'Repay hatred with Te'?" His answer: "How is one then to repay Te? Repay hatred with uprightness and repay Te with Te."[1] Lao Tzu's sage, however, knows of no hatred. He meets all men equally according to Tao, thus with Te.

The rest of the chapter shifts to the topic of how to deal with "big" (*ta*) and "difficult" (*nan*) matters. In so doing, it depicts the sage as the paragon of prudent planner and successful executor. What emerges here is a picture of the sage as a man of action (*wei*) or of affair (*shih*), rather than a man of "no-action" or of "no-affair." I suspect that these lines are probably an addition by a Legalist hand.[2]

Notes

[1]   *Analects*, 14: 36.

[2]   It may be worth noting that lines 6-11 are chosen for illustration in the Legalist text, the *Han Fei Tzu* (Ch. 21).

1   *What is at rest is easy to hold;*
2   *What has not yet shown its sign is easy to prepare for.*
3   *What is tender is easy to break up;*
4   *What is minute is easy to scatter.*
5   *Deal with things before they become reality;*
6   *Put things in order before disorder arises.*
7   *A tree as big as a man's embrace*
8   *Grows from the tip of a fine hair.*
9   *A terrace nine stories high*
10 *Rises from a heap of earth.*
11 *A journey of a thousand miles*
12 *Starts from where one stands.*
13 *Whoever acts on it will ruin it;*
14 *Whoever lays hold of it will lose it.*
15 *For this reason the sage*
16 *Does nothing and therefore ruins nothing;*
17 *Lays hold of nothing and therefore loses nothing.*
18 *People, in handling their affairs,*
19 *Always ruin their work on the verge of completion.*
20 *Be careful at the end as at the start,*
21 *And you will never fail.*
22 *For this reason the sage*
23 *Desires not to desire,*
24 *Does not treasure rare goods,*
25 *Learns not to learn.*
26 *He returns to what the multitude passes by.*
27 *He thus helps the ten thousand things to be so of themselves*
    [tzu jan],

28   *And does not try to rule.*

I hear two distinct voices speaking in this chapter: voice A in lines 1-12 and lines 18-21, and voice B in lines 13-17 and lines 22-28. It may be easy to see that the lines voiced by A are basically maxims for action (*wei*). In view of the fact that these lines are essentially precepts for successful action, they may be read as a continuation of the last portion of the previous chapter.

Let me put together, for clarity's sake, the interrupted voice B:

> Whoever acts [*wei*] on it will ruin it;
> Whoever lays hold of it will lose it.
> For this reason the sage
> Does nothing [*wu wei*] and therefore ruins
>   nothing;
> Lays hold of nothing and therefore loses nothing.
> For this reason the sage
> Desires not to desire,
> Does not treasure rare goods,
> Learns not to learn.
> He returns to what the multitude passes by.
> He thus helps the ten thousand things to be so
>   of themselves [*tzu jan*],
> And does not try to rule [*wei*].

This voice is clearly Lao Tzu's. The message in the first five lines (of voice B) is essentially the same as that of the opening lines of Chapter 60: "Governing a large state/ Is like boiling a small fish." One may find paradoxical the phrases "desires not to desire" and "learns not to learn." However, Lao Tzu's meaning is straightforward: the sage "desires nothing" and "learns nothing." There is obviously a word play in the two lines.[1]

What is that which "the multitude passes by" and "[the sage] returns to"? It is, of course, Tao.

Notes

[1]   In the Chinese text, lines 23 and 24 read: *yü pu yü/ hsüeh pu hsüeh.*

CHAPTER 65

1   *Of old a man who practiced Tao best*
2   *Did not thereby seek to make the people bright,*
3   *But to make them ignorant.*
4   *The people are difficult to govern,*
5   *Because they are too clever.*
6   *Therefore, to govern a state through knowledge*
7   *Is the robbing of the state;*
8   *Not to govern a state through knowledge*
9   *Is a blessing to the state.*
10   *Those who know these two*
11   *Also know the standard.*
12   *Always to know the standard*
13   *Is called the mysterious Te.*
14   *Deep and far-reaching is the mysterious Te!*
15   *Turn away from things.*
16   *Only then will the great obedience be attained.*

To make the people "ignorant" is to free them from all human learnings, so that they may return to Tao. To make the people "bright" is to teach them the way of civilization, thereby making them abandon Tao. That is why the man of Tao makes the people "ignorant."

By "great obedience" (*ta shun*) in the last line, Lao Tzu means submission to Tao. But to "obey" Tao is precisely to "turn away from things [of the human world]." Here, once again, he is calling for a transvaluation of the human universe.

CHAPTER 66

1   *The great rivers and seas are kings of hundred valleys,*
2   *Because they are good at keeping low.*
3   *That is why they can be kings of hundred valleys.*
4   *Therefore, if you want to stand above the people,*
5   *You must keep low in speaking to them.*
6   *If you want to stand ahead of the people,*
7   *You must put yourself behind them.*
8   *For this reason the sage*
9   *Is above the people yet does not weigh heavy on them;*
10 *He is ahead of the people yet causes no harm to them.*
11 *Therefore all under Heaven are happy to uphold him and never tire of him.*
12 *Because he does not contend,*
13 *No one under Heaven can contend with him.*

Lines 4-7 may sound somewhat paradoxical. They in effect tell the ambitious and self-centered to act unambitiously and selflessly—something that seems altogether impossible. But Lao Tzu's meaning is clear. To the ambitious, he is saying that they will not succeed in their pursuit. At the same time, he is announcing that only one who "keeps low in speaking to [the people]" and "puts himself behind them" will find himself above and ahead of others.

CHAPTER 67

1   *All under Heaven says that*
2   *My Tao is great yet doesn't look like it [Tao].*
3   *Truly, because it is great,*
4   *It doesn't look like it.*
5   *If it did,*
6   *It would have turned out a petty one long ago.*
7   *I have three treasures.*
8   *I hold and cherish them.*
9   *The first is called mercifulness;*
10 *The second, frugality;*
11 *The third, refusal to be ahead of all under Heaven.*
12 *Being merciful, you can therefore be brave;*
13 *Being frugal, you can therefore be liberal;*
14 *Refusing to be ahead of all under Heaven,*
15 *You can therefore become the leader of the vessels.*
16 *Now, to be brave, forsaking mercifulness,*
17 *To be liberal, forsaking frugality,*
18 *To be ahead, forsaking being behind*
19 *Is death.*
20 *With mercifulness—*
21 *If you fight, you will be triumphant,*
22 *If you defend, you will be invincible.*
23 *Whatever Heaven is about to save*
24 *Heaven will protect it with mercifulness.*

"My Tao" is infinite; therefore, it resembles no Tao people are familiar with. The sort of Tao they hear about, on the other hand, is necessarily finite, as it is necessarily taught in finite terms.

Only what is infinite is "great." Nothing finite is "great"; the name is its boundary.

Lao Tzu lists his "three treasures": "mercifulness," "frugality" and "refusal to be ahead of all under Heaven." The first makes one "brave," the second "liberal," and the third "the leader of the vessels."[1] Having said this, he adds: to be "brave" without "mercifulness," to be "liberal" without "frugality," and to be "ahead" without "being behind"—they all lead to "death." By contrast, the "three treasures" lead to life: They are virtues of life.

In the last five lines, Lao Tzu gives a special tribute to "mercifulness" (*tz'u*). Why this sudden praise of "mercifulness"? Hasn't he previously declared that "The sage is not humane [*jen*]" (Ch. 5)? What does he mean by *tz'u*? Is it different from the Confucian virtue of *jen* ("humaneness")? Is there any place for "mercifulness" in Lao Tzu's naturalistic universe? The character *tz'u* has appeared twice before,[2] in conjunction with *hsiao* ("filial piety"), meaning "parental love." It is used here alone, however, meaning more broadly "mercifulness"—a tender sentiment directed from "above" to "below."

In what sense can one say that this tender sentiment leads to bravery? Consider, for example, the bravery of an animal—especially a female—defending its young against an attacker. The source of the extraordinary courage of a tiny bird going after a huge bird of prey threatening its young is clearly its concern for the life of the young. Granted, we generally do not associate bravery with any tender sentiment like mercifulness. But how else can we explain the origin of such a daring act? Inasmuch as bravery without mercifulness means death,[3] one may say, bravery rooted in mercifulness is an affirmation of life. Mercifulness is a life-sentiment, a sort of biological sentiment without which no life of a species would be possible. It is perhaps only natural that this life-sentiment should be much stronger in the female than in the male. Lao Tzu's tribute to mercifulness once again reflects his perspective of the female, which is that of life. It is from this perspective of life that he says, "Being merciful, you can therefore be

brave"—the common association of "bravery" with
masculinity notwithstanding. He equates bravery with life
when it springs from the "softer" sex, but with death when it
comes from the "harder" sex.

In the last two lines, Lao Tzu speaks of Heaven's
"mercifulness." One may read them especially in view of his
universe, in which "the soft and weak prevails over the hard and
strong" (Ch. 36).[4] It is perhaps in this "prevailing" of the "weak"
over the "strong" that he sees Heaven's "mercifulness."

Notes

[1]   This phrase (*ch'i ch'ang*) is a variation of "chief of ministers" (*kuan ch'ang*) of
     Ch. 28. However, I read it to mean simply the leader of the people, rather
     than the head of government as chief administrator.

[2]   In Chs. 18, 19.

[3]   In Ch. 73, one reads: "Being brave in daring leads to death,/ Being brave in
     not daring leads to life."

[4]   See also Ch. 40, in which one reads: "Being weak is Tao's function."

CHAPTER 68

1   *A good warrior is not belligerent;*
2   *A good fighter is not given to anger;*
3   *One who is good at winning does not engage the enemy;*
4   *One who is good at using others takes the lower position.*
5   *This is called the Te of non-contention;*
6   *This is called making use of the strength of others;*
7   *This is called fit to be Heaven's mate.*
8   *It is the ultimate [truth] of old.*

Non-belligerence, non-contention, forbearance, passivity, and submissiveness—these are all female virtues. By describing a "good warrior," "good fighter" and so on, in terms of these virtues, Lao Tzu is, once again, pointing to the Te of the female. One who "holds fast to the female" is "fit to be Heaven's mate."

CHAPTER 69

1   *The strategists' saying:*
2   *"I dare not play the host but play the guest,*
3   *I dare not advance an inch but retreat a foot."*
4   *This is called marching no-marching,*
5   *Stretching no-arms,*
6   *Arming with no-weapons,*
7   *Charging at no-enemy.*
8   *No disaster is greater than making light of the enemy.*
9   *When I make light of the enemy, I may lose my treasure.*
10 *Therefore, when two sides confront each other with arms,*
11 *The one who grieves wins.*

The ostensible topic of this chapter is how best to fight and win. That is, however, not the real topic; fighting or winning is clearly something that would not interest Lao Tzu. Indeed, a good part of this passage, read as a guide to winning a war, would simply sound absurd. The real topic of the chapter is how not to fight or not to win. Here Lao Tzu teaches: the best way of fighting is no-fighting.

The saying cited at the outset points to the advantage of reacting rather than acting. The best way of responding to the aggressor is to "retreat." That is water's way. It is also the female's way of dealing with the male's aggression and activism.[1]

What is the meaning of the self-contradictory phrases in lines 4-7? Lao Tzu's paradoxical use of language here is nothing less than a subversion of language aimed at a transvaluation. We have seen his use of similar phrases many times before: for example, "relying on no-action," "practicing wordless teaching," "desiring no-desire," "learning no-learning," etc. However, the subversive nature of his paradoxical language seems particularly manifest in this chapter, as Lao Tzu repeatedly turns upside down the strategists' very universe, while offering to expound their maxim.

Read the last two lines: "Therefore, when two sides confront each other with arms,/ The one who grieves wins." "Grieving" at what? To be sure, at a mass slaughter about to take place. We have already read the following lines (Ch. 31):

> Having committed mass killings [at war].
> Let us weep with deep sorrow;
> For a victory, let us observe funeral rites.

"Grieving" has, of course, nothing to do with winning or losing. Nor is Lao Tzu interested in who wins and who loses. From the standpoint of civilization, his declaration that the "grieving" party wins sounds irrelevant, even absurd. Wartime is no time for "grief"; it's a time to kill! Lao Tzu's absurdity or irrelevance demonstrates the extent to which human civilization has turned away from Tao, life's way.

Notes

[1] Recall the following line from Ch. 61: "The female always overcomes the male by stillness."

CHAPTER 70

1   *My words are very easy to understand,*
2   *Very easy to put into practice.*
3   *Yet no one under Heaven can understand them*
4   *Or put them into practice.*
5   *Words have their source,*
6   *Deeds have their lord.*
7   *Truly, because people don't know this,*
8   *They don't understand me.*
9   *Those who know me are few;*
10   *Those who follow me are rare.*[1]
11   *For this reason the sage*
12   *Wears coarse cloth but carries jade inside.*

"My words are very easy to understand,/ Very easy to put into practice." But why is it that people neither "understand them" nor "put them into practice"? Because they are unable to go beyond "words" or "deeds." "Words" have their spring, and "deeds" their cause. People, however, recognize neither the "source" of "my" words nor the "lord" of "my" deeds, namely, Tao. Is Tao then hard to "understand" or to "put into practice"? No. Tao is within reach of anyone who turns away from the man-made universe and returns to nature (*tzu-jan*). Indeed, Tao *is* life, and *I am* it, as *I* live it.

Notes

[1]   I follow Fukunaga's reading of *kuei*. See Fukunaga, Vol. 2, p. 165.

1 *To know yet not to know is best;*
2 *Not to know yet to know is a disease.*
3 *Truly, when you recognize a disease as a disease,*
4 *You are free of disease.*
5 *The sage is free of disease.*
6 *Because he recognizes a disease as a disease,*
7 *He is free of disease.*

(The poetry of this chapter is evident in the original.[1] It may best be read as a poem. Any literal or analytic reading of the lines would be inappropriate.)

The first two lines may be paraphrased as follows: To know yet not to think that one knows is best; not to know yet to think that one knows is a disease.

Recognize your ignorance as ignorance. Once you are aware of your ignorance, you are free from it. This, of course, does not mean that you now know what you did not know previously. It simply means that you are free of the "disease" of ignorance, namely, of the illusion of knowledge. The sage is free of this "disease," because he recognizes it. But more correctly, the disease never touches him, because he is above both knowledge and ignorance, in the first place. He is indeed one who knows yet does not think that he knows.

Notes

[1] No attempt is made here to convey its music in English. The following transliteration may give the reader some sense of its poetry:

151

chih pu chih shang
pu chih chih ping
fu wei ping ping
shih i pu ping
sheng jen pu ping
i ch'i ping ping
shih i pu ping.

Note that each line consists of four characters, and all lines, except line 1, end with *ping*, which occur altogether 8 times. Notice also the contrasting sounds of *chih pu chih* and *pu chih chih*, and of *ping ping* and *pu ping*.

CHAPTER 72

1 *When the people do not fear the authority [of the sovereign],*
2 *The supreme authority arrives.*
3 *They are neither contented in their abodes,*[1]
4 *Nor satisfied with their lives.*
5 *Only because they are not satisfied,*
6 *They cannot be suppressed.*
7 *Therefore the sage*
8 *Knows himself but does not show himself,*
9 *Cherishes himself but does not exalt himself.*
10 *Therefore he discards that and takes this.*

"The supreme authority" [*ta wei*] means the "authority" of Heaven. Accordingly, the first two lines mean: When the people cease to "fear" the "authority" of the sovereign, Heaven's punishment visits the land. Heaven's displeasure is, of course, the worst thing that can happen, not only to the people but also to the ruler himself. Who is to be blamed for Heaven's punishment? None but the ruler. The people's attitude toward the ruler merely reflects how he rules.

I read the next four lines (3-6) as a description of the people's discontent under the rule of a sovereign they no longer "fear."[2] Why their discontent? Because they are driven by their insatiable desires. Once these desires are aroused, no sovereign "authority" can "suppress" them. The people's unbridled desires only lead to social chaos, violence, and universal misery.

Here, Lao Tzu returns to his topic of reducing the people's desires—the primary concern of the sage. How does the sage free them of their man-made desires? By "not showing himself" and "not exalting himself." Such is his "wordless teaching."

Notes

[1]   It is common to read *hsia* to mean "to make narrow." But I follow here Fukunaga. See Fukunaga, Vol. 2, p. 171.

[2]   I read them especially in light of Lao Tzu's ideal state depicted in Ch. 80.

CHAPTER 73

1   *Being brave in daring leads to death,*
2   *Being brave in not daring leads to life.*
3   *Of these two,*
4   *One is advantageous and the other injurious.*
5   *What Heaven detests—*
6   *Who knows its reason?*
7   *Therefore even the sage finds it hard to tell.*
8   *The way of Heaven—*
9   *It never contends yet is good at winning,*
10 *It never speaks yet is good at responding.*
11 *It comes of itself without being invited,*
12 *It seems remiss yet good at planning.*
13 *Heaven's net is vast.*
14 *Though its meshes are coarse, nothing escapes it.*

"Daring" (*kan*) means male activism, whereas "not daring" means female passivity. The former leads to death, and the latter to life.[1]

Heaven detests contention. Nobody knows why, not even the sage. Is it because Heaven's "reason" (*ku*) is beyond man's comprehension?

Heaven "wins" without contending, "responds" without a word, "comes" without being asked to, and "plans" without calculating. These are all "perfect" acts—like "perfect going" (which "leaves no tracks"), "perfect speech" (which "leaves no flecks"), and "perfect counting" (which "uses no counters") (Ch. 27). Heaven's "winning" is "no-winning," its "responding" "no-responding," its "coming" "no-coming," and its "planning" "no-planning."

"Heaven's net" (*t'ien wang*) in the penultimate line is sometimes understood to mean the "net" to catch "evil" people.[2] But Heaven makes no distinction between "good" and "evil." In this respect, the law of nature understood in science comes close to Lao Tzu's idea of *t'ien wang*. Note his naturalistic view of nature (*tzu-jan*).

Notes

[1]   See my comment on Ch. 67.
[2]   See, e.g., Fukunaga, Vol. 2, p. 175.

CHAPTER 74

1   *When the people do not fear death,*
2   *How can you frighten them with death?*
3   *Suppose the people do always fear death,*
4   *And we can seize and kill*
5   *Those who are lawless.*
6   *But who would dare to do so?*
7   *There is always the one who administers killings, and he does the killing.*
8   *If you do the killing, taking his place,*
9   *This is called hewing wood taking the place of the master-carpenter.*
10 *If you hew wood taking the place of the master-carpenter,*
11 *You will seldom escape injuring your own hand.*

Here we read Lao Tzu's argument against capital punishment. The ruler threatens the people with death to keep them from doing wrong things. But better not. For people either fear or do not fear death. In the latter case, no threat will work. In the former case, a threat to kill may work. But, by threatening to kill, the ruler will be presuming Heaven's function, thus, putting himself at the risk of punishment from above. By the "one who administers killings" Lao Tzu means the ultimate dispenser of death, namely, Heaven. Capital punishment amounts to punishing a human being by killing on behalf of Heaven. But who would dare to act, "taking [Heaven's] place"? Who would presume to know Heaven's will? Life and death belong only to Heaven.

CHAPTER 75

1 *The people starve*
2 *Because the ruler consumes too much tax-grain.*
3 *Because of this they starve.*
4 *The people are hard to govern*
5 *Because the ruler rules through action [yu* wei*],*
6 *Because of this they are hard to govern.*
7 *The people take their death lightly*
8 *Because the ruler hoards his life.*
9 *Because of this they take their death lightly.*
10 *Truly, one who does nothing with life*
11 *Is wiser than one who prizes [the value of] life.*

To "rule through action" is to govern against nature. That is why "the people are hard to govern."

The ruler "hoards his life" at the expense of his people. That is why they "take their death lightly."

In the last two lines, Lao Tzu rejects the very foundation of civilization, which is his ultimate subversion. By "one who does nothing with life," he means one who *simply* lives, without attempting to accomplish anything (name) with his life. Such a one lives in immediacy, in the nameless. On the other hand, "one who prizes [the value of] life" is one who seeks to achieve something *meaningful* with his life. He lives in the civilized world of meanings and values. For him some lives are more valuable and hence worth pursuing than others. In his eyes, indeed, the "nameless" life of immediacy is despicable, hardly distinguishable from animal existence. By announcing that of these two types the first is "wiser" than the second, Lao Tzu is subverting the very premise of civilization: namely, the proposition that life of immediacy is not worth living, and man ought to live a *meaningful* life.

One may ask here, But isn't the man of no-action precisely one who "does nothing with life"?[1] Isn't he one who lives in immediacy, having returned to the nameless state of *p'u*? Does this mean that Lao Tzu is teaching, after all, life *devoid of* meaning? Is this what his naturalistic view of life leads to? The answer to each of these questions has to be yes, insofar as the man who lives in immediacy does not seek a "meaningful" life. Note, however: neither does he seek a "meaningless" life. The question of the "meaning" of life simply does not arise at the level of immediacy. Only the civilized, those meaning-bound, raise such questions.

Notes

[1] I take the phrase "does nothing [with life]" (*wu [i sheng] wei*) in line 10 in the sense of *wu-wei* (no-action). Compare Lao Tzu's attitude toward life with Confucius's reflected in the following episode in the *Analects* (14:46):

> Yüan Jang was squatting on his heels, watching the Master [Confucius] approach. The Master said: "When young, showing no respect to the elders; when grown up, doing nothing worth mentioning; when old, living on without dying—this is a thief [of life]." So saying, he lightly hit the man on the shin with his staff.

Isn't it possible that Yüan Jang was none other than a Taoist recluse?

CHAPTER 76

1   *People are soft and weak when born,*
2   *But hard and strong when dead.*
3   *Plants are soft and supple when born,*[1]
4   *But dry and shriveled when dead.*
5   *Therefore the hard and strong are companions of death,*
6   *The soft and weak are companions of life.*
7   *Therefore a strong weapon loses,*
8   *A strong tree breaks.*
9   *The strong and big belong below,*
10   *The soft and weak belong above.*

In this chapter one reads once again Lao Tzu's tribute to the "soft and weak."

Note that the world outlook expressed in these lines is fundamentally naturalistic or even biological: it is neither moral nor aesthetic. Not that the "hard and strong" are evil, and the "soft and weak" good; nor that the "hard and strong" are ugly, and the "soft and weak" beautiful. Rather, "the hard and strong are companions of death," and "the soft and weak are companions of life."

Notes

[1] The standard text has *wan wu* ("ten thousand things") before *ts'ao mu* ("plants"). But I omit *wan wu*, following Lau's emendation. See *Lau*, pp. 118, 192.

CHAPTER 77

1   *The way of Heaven—*
2   *Isn't it like stretching a bow?*
3   *You press down the high,*
4   *Raise the low,*
5   *Take away the excess,*
6   *Add to the deficient.*
7   *The way of Heaven*
8   *Takes away from those who have too much and gives to those who have not enough.*
9   *The way of man*
10   *Is not so.*
11   *It takes away from those who have not enough and offers to those who have too much.*
12   *Who can have too much and offer to all under Heaven?*
13   *Only the man of Tao can.*
14   *Therefore the sage*
15   *Rules without depending on anyone.*
16   *His work is done, but he never dwells in it.*
17   *He does not wish to show his worthiness.*

In this chapter Lao Tzu contrasts the "way of Heaven" with the "way of man."

"The way of Heaven" is Tao. That is why Heaven "takes away from those who have too much and gives to those who have not enough." Tao is the "nursing mother" of all, the "sanctuary of the ten thousand things." Tao is fair. So is Heaven. Its fairness arises from its motherly nature.[1]

But the "way of man" is the opposite, because he relentlessly pursues values of his own making. Man wants glory, power, name, wealth, etc., never knowing when to stop. So man "takes away from those who have not enough and offers to those who have too much."[2]

"Who can have too much and offer to all under Heaven?/ Only the man of Tao can." Of what has he "too much"? Te. Thanks to his superabundance of Te," he benefits all under Heaven.

Notes

[1] Recall Lao Tzu's ascription of "mercifulness" to Heaven in Ch. 67.

[2] Isn't this the capitalist's way? If so, how far removed the capitalist's idea of *laissez-faire* is from nature's way (Tao)—contrary to the claim of its advocates!

CHAPTER 78

1   *Nothing under Heaven is softer and weaker than water.*
2   *Yet in attacking what is hard and strong*
3   *Nothing can surpass water,*
4   *Because nothing can destroy it.*[1]
5   *That the weak prevails over the strong,*
6   *That the soft prevails over the hard—*
7   *This everyone under Heaven knows,*
8   *Yet none can practice it.*
9   *Therefore the sage says:*
10   *"He who takes on himself the shame of the state*
11   *Is called lord of the land*[2];
12   *He who takes on himself the misfortune of the state*
13   *Is called king of all under Heaven."*
14   *True words sound contrary.*

One "practices" the prevailing of the weak over the strong by practicing the female virtues of passivity and non-contention. No wonder that few practice it in the male-dominant universe!

Who can assume upon himself the "shame" and "misfortune" of the state? Only one who "holds fast to the female." He will become "lord of the land" and "king of all under Heaven." Recall the following lines from Chapter 28: "Know the male,/ Hold fast to the female,/ And you will become the ravine of all under Heaven."

Notes

[1]   I follow Morohashi's reading. See Morohashi, p. 148.
[2]   Literally, "lord of the shrine of land and grain."

163

CHAPTER 79

1   *You allay the great discontent,*
2   *Yet, surely, there will still remain some discontent.*
3   *How can this be considered good?*
4   *Therefore the sage*
5   *Holds the left-hand tally,*
6   *Makes no claims on the people.*
7   *The man of Te oversees the tally,*
8   *The man of no Te oversees tax-collection.*
9   *The way of Heaven favors none,*
10   *Always sides with the good man.*

This chapter has been interpreted in various ways, mainly because of the uncertain use of such phrases as "great discontent," "overseeing the tally" and "overseeing tax-collection."[1] I read it basically as a passage addressed to the rulers, urging them to be lenient rather than exacting.

"Great discontent" (*ta yüan*) means the people's "discontent" under harsh government. An oppressive ruler may sometimes—whether out of necessity or sheer whim—take actions in order to placate his people. What "good" would such passing measures do to dispel their deep-rooted "discontent"?

In antiquity the Chinese used tallies for business transactions.[2] For purposes of accounting, the creditor kept the left half and the debtor the right half of the tally.[3] Here, referring to the sage as the one who "holds the left-hand tally," Lao Tzu is presenting him as a "creditor" with a sort of unspoken contract with the people—a contract of ruling in which the ruler is benefactor and the ruled, beneficiary. As creditor or benefactor vis-à-vis the people, the sage gives them life and nurtures them. Yet he "makes no claims on the people."

In lines 7-8, Lao Tzu contrasts the overriding concern of the one who rules through Te and that of the one who rules without Te. The former "oversees the tally," namely, his contract of ruling, while the latter "oversees tax-collection," namely, his granary.[4] No wonder that the latter should face the "great discontent" of his people.

Notes

[1] See e.g. different translations of these phrases by Waley, Chan and Lau.

[2] See for the use of tallies in ancient China Waley, p. 256 ("Additional Notes").

[3] See Fukunaga, Vol. 2, p. 194.

[4] The Chou government used a system of tithe, called *ch'e*, which I translate here as "tax-collection." See Fukunaga, Vol. 2, p. 195.

CHAPTER 80

1   *Let the state be small and its people few.*
2   *Let the thousand contrivances go idle.*
3   *Let the people take death seriously and not move to distant places.*
4   *Though they may have boats and carriages,*
5   *They will not ride in them.*
6   *Though they may have armor and weapons,*
7   *They will not display them.*
8   *Let the people return to the practice of knotting cords.*
9   *They will relish what they eat,*
10 *Find their clothes beautiful,*
11 *Be content in their homes,*
12 *Delight in their customs.*
13 *States may be within sight of one another,*
14 *So that one may hear cocks and dogs from a neighboring state;*
15 *Yet people will grow old and die*
16 *Without trafficking with another state.*

Here we read Lao Tzu's description of what might be called his ideal village-state: a peaceful, idyllic community. Why does he propose or, rather, dream of, such a community? What sort of wellbeing does he envision for its people? One may answer these questions especially in view of Lao Tzu's time, namely, the Warring States period (403-221 B.C.), which was the climax of centuries-long struggles among contending powers prior to the first unification of China. Lao Tzu's ideal community was in a way a dream born from this historical condition, a dream that reflected the fervent longings of the suffering people—above all, their longing for a universal peace. In this chapter he describes his vision of a community where this dream may be realized. What he presents here is a community of simple wellbeing in which every man and woman would be left alone to enjoy and complete his or her Heaven-appointed life.

"Let the state be small and the people few," so that it will not dare aspire to conquer all under Heaven. It is large and powerful states that harbor such an ambition and engage in constant warfare.

In line 2 and lines 4-7, Lao Tzu is explicit in rejecting the fruits of human technology. Notice especially his mention of "boats and carriages" and "armor and weapons"—all instruments of civilization.

Why does Lao Tzu say: "Let the people take death seriously"? To take death seriously is to take life seriously. But how can the people take their life seriously when the ruler thinks nothing of sacrificing tens of thousands of them?

In line 8, he speaks of "the practice of knotting cords." This refers to the use of knotted ropes as a device for record-keeping in prehistoric China.[1] Let the people return to simple life close to nature.

What kind of life, then, does Lao Tzu allow his people to enjoy?

> They will relish what they eat,
> Find their clothes beautiful,
> Be content in their homes,
> Delight in their customs.

Notes

[1] See Waley, p. 241; Fukunaga, Vol. 2, p. 202.

Chapter 81

1   *Trustworthy words are not beautiful,*
2   *Beautiful words are not trustworthy.*
3   *The good are not eloquent,*
4   *The eloquent are not good.*
5   *The wise are not learned,*
6   *The learned are not wise.*
7   *The sage stocks up nothing.*
8   *After using for others what he has,*
9   *He finds himself with still more.*
10 *After giving to others what he has,*
11 *He finds his stock even greater.*
12 *The way of Heaven*
13 *Is to benefit and not to harm.*
14 *The way of the sage*
15 *Is to rule and not to contend.*

This final chapter hardly needs comments. I give here its transliteration in order to convey some sense of its music/poetry, which is evident in the original text.

A.   (lines 1-2)   *hsin yüan pu mei/ mei yüan pu hsin*
       (lines 3-4)   *shan che pu pien/ pien che pu shan*
       (lines 5-6)   *chih che pu po/ po che pu chih*
B.   (line 7)   *sheng jen pu chi*
C.   (lines 8-9)   *chi i wei jen/ chi yü yu*
       (lines 10-11) *chi i yü jen/ chi yü to*
D.   (lines 12-13) *t'ien chih tao/ li erh pu hai*
       (lines 14-15) *sheng-jen chih tao/ wei erh pu cheng*[1]

Notes

1 Notice the following recurring patterns in this transliteration: (I am using the symbol "~" to indicate the occurrence of the negative particle *pu*.)

A: *a, b, ~ c/ c, b, ~ a.*

C: *a, b, c, d/ e, f, g.* (In lines 8-9 and lines 10-11, different characters occur only in two places, *c* and *g*, all the rest remaining identical.)

D: *a, b, c/ d, e, ~ f.* (In line 14 the compound word *sheng-jen* ["sage"] appears in *a*, which corresponds to *t'ien* ["Heaven"] in line 12. Notice also the recurring sounds of *chih tao* and *erh pu* in lines 12-13 and lines 14-15.)

APPENDIX I

LAO TZU AND CONFUCIUS

One peculiar feature of the *Tao Te Ching* is that it never mentions any personal names. However, there is no question that its central teachings are aimed precisely against Confucius. Our dating of the work places the appearance of the bulk of the text more than a century after the death of Confucius.[1] By this time his teachings had already become the dominant ideology of China, and it was with the backdrop of this ideology that the *Tao Te Ching* came into existence. It is for this reason that many of its passages often gain added intelligibility when they are read especially against Confucius's sayings. In this Appendix, I discuss the contrasting views of Lao Tzu and Confucius on certain key subjects.

1.

Underlying Confucius's ethical thought is the idea that human beings in the state of nature are essentially indistinguishable from animals and therefore must be made *human* through learning. Hence, his emphasis on education. In this respect, his teachings may be summed up in one word: humanization. His ideal man, "noble man" (*chün-tzu*), is none other than one who has overcome his low (animal) nature. In one of his sayings in the *Analects*, Confucius says: "Let there be education; there is no distinction from birth" (15:38). Another saying: "By nature [*hsing*] men are alike. Through practice they become far apart" (17:2). His imperative of humanization is explicit in the following saying: "To overcome oneself and submit to ritual propriety [*li*] is to practice humaneness [*jen*]" (12:1). Indeed, humaneness is the very heart of Confucian ethics. To "practice humaneness (*jen*)" is to be

173

truly *human*. But how does one "practice *jen*"? Only by learning the rules of propriety (*li*) and practicing it. Thus, the opening saying of the *Analects* (1:1): "To learn and practice from time to time what one has learned, is that not after all a pleasure?"

For Confucius, Tao is the way of living *as* a (true) human being. And this way (Tao) turns out to be the ritual tradition of antiquity,[2] for humaneness may be cultivated and practiced only according to the established rules of propriety (*li*). He professes: "I transmit [the way of old], but do not invent. I believe in and love the ancients" (7:1).[3]

In the *Analects*, one of Confucius's disciples remarks: "We could hear the Master speak on culture [*wen chang*], but could not hear him speak on human nature [*hsing*] and the way of Heaven [*t'ien tao*]" (5:12). This remark is significant because it reveals Confucius's total devotion to tradition or the human way, and, at the same time, his lack of interest in "the way of Heaven," the subject of supreme importance for Lao Tzu. *Wen chang* represents the distinctly human universe of tradition, while *t'ien tao* refers to the way of the larger universe beyond, the cosmos. As a matter of fact, Confucius himself never mentions *t'ien tao* anywhere. By contrast, one finds the same term (and its close variant *t'ien chih tao*) appear several times in the *Tao Te Ching*.[4] For Lao Tzu, "the way of Heaven" means, of course, none other than Tao, the way of nature.

To say that Confucius never spoke of *t'ien tao* is not to suggest that he avoided the idea of Tao altogether. In fact, the term Tao appears quite frequently in the *Analects*. Yet, for him it always signifies the uniquely human way—the exact opposite of what Lao Tzu means by it. In an oft-cited saying, Confucius says: "Man can broaden Tao; it is not that Tao can broaden man" (15:28). For him there is no Tao to be found outside the human world of names and values. Here we see the fundamental difference between Confucius and Lao Tzu: Confucius's ethical or humanistic view of Tao versus Lao Tzu's naturalistic view of Tao.[5]

Lao Tzu opens the *Tao Te Ching* with an announcement of

the unspeakability and, hence, unteachability of Tao. Indeed, there is a mutual implication between his denial of Tao's teachability, on the other hand, and his central teachings such as the nameless Tao, the mysterious Te and wordless teaching. By contrast, observe Confucius's faith in, or rather, assumption of, the teachability of Tao, which is evident in his numerous sayings stressing the importance of education (*chiao*) and learning (*hsüeh*).[6] This faith is perhaps quite understandable in view of his trust in the human universe of names[7] as well as in light of his conception of Tao as the *human* way. There is a logical connection between Confucius's humanistic view of Tao, on the one hand, and his faith in its teachability, on the other, just as there is an inseparable relation between Lao Tzu's rejection of the name-mediated human universe, on the one hand, and his idea of the unspeakable and unteachable Tao, on the other.

2.

Next, let us look at the radically different conceptions of sage (*sheng jen*) or sagehood (*sheng*) taught by the two philosophers. For both the sage is the personification of Tao. However, for one he is the *human* way incarnate and for the other the way of *nature* incarnate. Confucius says: "A sage [*sheng jen*] I cannot expect to meet. I will be happy to meet a noble man [*chün-tzu*]" (7:25). For him the sage is the ethical archetype the "noble man" ought to emulate: he is humane (*jen*), wise (*chih*) and righteous (*i*). But this ethical idea of sage is precisely what Lao Tzu has in mind in the following lines (Ch. 19):

> Banish sagehood and wisdom,
> And the people will benefit a hundredfold.
> Banish humaneness and righteousness,
> And the people will return to filial piety and
> parental love.

For Confucius the sage is, above all, humane (*jen*). So, in one saying (7:33), he speaks of "sagehood" (*sheng*) and "humaneness" (*jen*) in one breath: "As to sagehood and humaneness, how can I even aspire to realize them?" Now, read the following lines from Lao Tzu:

> Heaven and Earth are not humane [*pu jen*];
> They treat the ten thousand things as straw
> dogs.
> The sage is not humane [*pu jen*];
> He treats the people as straw dogs. (Ch. 5)

Just as both men regard the sage as the embodiment of Tao, so they both speak of the sage ruler as the one who governs through his Te—the power of Tao. But they do so, again, in two diametrically opposite ways. For Lao Tzu, the sage exercises Te according to *nature*'s way, so that his leadership is invisible to his people. His Te is "mysterious." And the people call his leadership "*tzu-jan.*" On the other hand, for Confucius the sage's Te is essentially moral power, power that he exercises by acting (*wei*) according to the *human* way: that is, in compliance with ritual tradition (*li*). His is thus moral leadership, which must be visible, so that the people may follow his example. Confucius says:

> If you lead the people through regulations [*cheng*] and keep order by punishments [*hsing*], they will avoid them and have no sense of shame. If you lead them through Te and keep order by the practice of ritual propriety [*li*], they will have a sense of shame and also set themselves right. (2:3

Significantly, Confucius, too, asserts that the sage governs through no-action. He says:

One who governed through no-action [*wu-wei*]—wasn't Shun[8] such a one? What action [*wei*] did he take? All he did was to place himself on the throne, facing south respectfully. (15:4)[9]

(Note: "Facing south" here refers to the sovereign's *correct* position on the throne, implying Shun's compliance with ritual or ceremonial tradition [*li*].)

For Lao Tzu, however, ritual rules (*li*) are no more than man-made conventions, which he rejects. In fact, he regards the man of *li* as a man of action (*yu-wei*) rather than of no-action (*wu-wei*), along with the man of humaneness (*jen*) and the man of righteousness (*i*).[10] Probably, he may even grant that Shun was a man of moral virtue (Te in the Confucian sense). But he would say Shun was still a man of "inferior Te," insofar as he *acted* (as a moral agent). "A man of superior Te never acts" (Ch. 38).

According to Confucius, the sage (or the *chün-tzu*) is the one who leads the people out of their natural state and bring them into the ethical and ritualized universe; in short, his task is to humanize or civilize people. By contrast, Lao Tzu envisions the sage leading the people precisely in the opposite direction: that is, out of the human universe of names and values, and back to the state of *p'u*, to the nameless life of nature.

I earlier quoted two sayings of Confucius that stress the importance of education. Let me cite two more here:

Only when men of good character have taught people for seven years, can they be allowed to bear arms. (13:29
To send people to war without having first taught them is to abandon them. (13:30)

For Confucius people ought to be "taught" even to go to war. Why? Because war, too, is an organized, human enterprise which only those trained or civilized are capable of carrying out. On the other hand, what does Lao Tzu say about educating the people ("making the people bright")?

> Of old a man who practiced Tao best
> Did not thereby seek to make the people bright,
> But to make them ignorant.
> The people are difficult to govern,
> Because they are too clever.
> Therefore, to govern a state through knowledge
> Is the robbing of the state;
> Not to govern a state through knowledge
> Is a blessing to the state. (Ch. 65

Isn't Lao Tzu here opposing Confucius's idea of education as the task of government? For one thing, his sage would not make the people "bright" to send them to war.

3.

We have considered how opposed Lao Tzu and Confucius are on such subjects as Tao, Te, the sage, moral leadership and education. As I close this discussion, however, I would like to note that their opposing positions were two radically different attempts to deal with the same historical reality: namely, the many centuries of social and political turmoil, warfare, and the accompanying human sufferings that had been afflicting the Middle Kingdom. Both philosophers aimed at ending that state of affairs and establishing a universal peace (t'ai-p'ing). In the same reality one saw the unhappy consequences of human civilization and the need for return to the Tao of nature, while the other saw the decline of the ritual tradition of antiquity and the need for restoration of the *human* way (Tao) through the overcoming of nature.

One may be inclined to ask, Whose view is right, Lao Tzu's or Confucius's? I think the question is inappropriate. For the two views only represent two different ways of looking at the world—though, to be sure, they do entail radically different existential attitudes toward life. According to Ssu-ma Ch'ien, Lao Tzu lived in Chou (the royal domain of the Chou king) for a long time but departed after seeing its decline. I find this legend quite fitting in view of Lao Tzu's teachings. Contrast his withdrawal from the human world[11] with Confucius's lifelong efforts to reverse the tide of history—a tireless devotion that equally befits *his* teachings. Isn't the contrast one between a man of nature (pre- or post-ethical man) and a man of man (an ethical man)?

Notes

[1]   See Introduction.

[2]   Namely, the "way of the Former Kings." See *Analects*, 1:12.

[3]   In another saying (15:30) he says: "Once I spent a whole day without food and a whole night without sleep, in thinking, but it did no good. It is better to learn."

[4]   E.g.: Chs. 9, 47, 73.

[5]   The difference between Confucius's concept of Tao and Lao Tzu's has generally been recognized by various commentators. For a succinct statement of the difference, see Graham, p. 13.

[6]   Perhaps the ultimate testimony to that faith is his life devoted to learning and teaching. In his old age, Confucius traveled for fourteen years on end in search of rulers receptive to his teachings, but without success. In contrast to Confucius's devotion to teaching, it is remarkable that, in spite of the exaggerated legend of Lao Tzu, there is only one episode of his giving an instruction to anyone, and this happens to be the story of his admonition to Confucius, who had sought to be instructed on matters of *li* (ritual propriety). Ssu-ma Ch'ien records that Lao Tzu begun his reply by saying: "You are talking about those who have long decomposed along with their bones, leaving behind only their words."

[7]   Confucius's faith in the universe of "names" (*ming*) is perhaps best revealed in his teaching of "rectification of names." In one saying, one

of his pupils asks him what he would do before anything else if he should be invited by the ruler of Wei to govern his state. His reply: "It would certainly be to correct names [*cheng ming*]" (13:3). Failing to grasp his meaning, the disciple protests that names have nothing to do with government. In his response, Confucius tells him in essence that when the use of names (language) becomes corrupt, it will result in the decline of ritual [*li*] as well as in the misapplication of punishment, and that when this happens, "the people will find nowhere to put hand and foot."

[8]   Shun is one of the three legendary sage kings of ancient China.

[9]   Read also the following saying (2:1): "He who rules by Te may be compared to the pole-star, which keeps its place, while the multitude of stars do homage to it." In his comment on this sayings, Chan writes that "Confucianism and Taoism are in agreement" on the principle of "government by virtue [*te*]" and the idea of "government through inaction [*wu-wei*]." (See Chan [1963a], p. 22.) I fear he is mistaken here.

[10]   See Ch. 38, where Lao Tzu gives especially a humorous portrayal of a man of *li*: "A man of superior ritual propriety [*li*] acts [*wei*];/ And when others fail to respond accordingly,/ He stretches his arm and charges at them."

[11]   After leaving Chou, according to the legend, Lao Tzu reaches the mountain pass (Han-ku Kuan?), where he is entreated by the gate keeper to write a book for his sake. It is upon this request that he writes what is now known as *Tao Te Ching*. Thereafter he continues his journey. Ssu-ma Ch'ien writes: "No one knows how he ended his life."

APPENDIX II

THE SAGE, THE ENLIGHTENED ONE

The term "sage" (*sheng jen*) occurs in the *Tao Te Ching* almost as frequently as the term Tao. In most of these occurrences, Lao Tzu speaks of the sage as the ideal ruler. However, there are several passages in which the sage emerges as the "enlightened" one. The sage "knows the constant," namely, Tao. Lao Tzu calls this "knowing of the constant [*ch'ang*]" *ming,* rather than *chih* ("wisdom").[1] To be in the state of *ming* is to be "enlightened" or to be "in the light."[2] One may be "wise" (*chih*) but may still "be greatly deluded," that is, in the dark.[3] There are several instances in which he refers to the sage's perspicacity by the term *ming,* where its underlying sense of being "in the light" is unmistakable.[4] (In my translation, I have rendered the character *ming* variously, depending on its context, sometimes as "light," sometimes as "enlightenment," sometimes as "bright," and sometimes as "clear sight.")

To be "enlightened" or "in the light" is to "know." But this knowing is unlike name-mediated, human knowing; it is certainly not intellectual knowing. That is why one may be "wise" (*chih*) in matters concerning the visible, human world, but may still be utterly in the dark about the realm beyond, the invisible.[5] To be in the state of *ming* is to see, to be aware of, what is imperceptible to the name-bound, human faculties. So Lao Tzu once calls this perspicacity "subtle light" (*wei ming*).[6] In another place, he says: "To see what is small is called clear sight [*ming*]."[7]

In Chapter 10, one reads: "As bright light [*ming pai*] reaches all four directions,/ Can you remain unknowing?" This passage is particularly indicative of how Lao Tzu views the sage's direct (unmediated) perspicaciousness. By *ming pai* I take him to mean a certain state of awareness: namely, awareness of the present, illuminated by unobstructed light. It is that immediate awareness in which the sage sees the nameless, the present, under the aspect of Tao. One attains this awareness, however, only by freeing oneself of all name-mediated, human knowledge.

The sage is "enlightened" (*ming*), as he is immediately aware of "the constant" in the present. It is ultimately this awareness that makes him altogether different from all other living beings. The sage lives a nameless life, as he lives in immediacy. So does every living being in nature. But the wild lack consciousness. Hence, their darkness.[8] Unlike these creatures of nature, humans have consciousness.[9] For common humanity, however, this consciousness is bound to the visible domain and thus unable to reach the nameless. Hence, its darkness.

The sage sees the present under the aspect of Tao. What does this mean, in concrete terms? I find an illuminating instance of such a "seeing" (*kuan*) in the following passage (Ch. 16):

> Attain the utmost emptiness [*hsü*],
> Hold fast to stillness [*ching*].
> The ten thousand things rise together;
> I see [*kuan*] them return.
> All things flourish;
> Each reverts to its root.
> Reverting to the root is called stillness.
> It means submission to fate.
> Submission to fate is called [submission to] the
> constant.
> To know the constant is called enlightenment.

The phrase "I see" in the fourth line clearly announces the presence of *awareness* on the part of the speaker. It is quite appropriate that Lao Tzu closes these lines by declaring: "To know the constant [*ch'ang*] is called enlightenment [*ming*]."

This quoted passage is revealing also in another respect. I have in mind particularly the first two lines. As I read them, they indicate the very *condition* of being "enlightened." To "attain the utmost emptiness [*hsü*]" means to release one's mind (or awareness) from all thoughts and thus to reach absolute "stillness" (*ching*). This state of "emptiness" and "stillness" is precisely the condition of "enlightenment." Without "emptiness," no "stillness"; without "stillness," no "light." I want to stress here the importance of freeing one's mind of all desires—not only of abstract desires but also of the body's desires.[10]

In the second part of Chapter 1, one reads the following lines: "Therefore, always free of desire [*wu yü*], you see [*kuan*] the secret;/ Always with desire [*yu yü*] you see [*kuan*] its appearance." Here we have one of the first stumbling blocks of the *Tao Te Ching* for many of its readers. What has being "free of desire" to do with the "seeing of the secret"? The answer may be clear, as long as one keeps in mind freedom from desires—namely, "emptiness" and "stillness"—as the condition of "being in the light." To be able to "see [*kuan*] the secret,"[11] one must be "in the light" (*ming*). But to be "in the light" is to be "free of desire."

A final note. I have so far discussed how only the sage, of all creatures, sees "in the light." Does this mean that his place in the universe is unique on that account, and that he, for that reason, occupies a special, or even a higher, place among all things of nature? The answer has to be no. Here one may be reminded of the opening lines of Chapter 19: "Banish sagehood [*sheng*] and wisdom [*chih*],/ And the people will benefit a hundredfold." The crucial point is that sagehood, too, is nothing more than a *name*, which has its meaning only as the correlative of its opposite, namely, common humanity. The "sage," too, like ordinary mortals, exists only in the human universe of names, and neither in nature nor in the sage's eyes. *Under the aspect of Tao*, there is no distinction between sage and common mortal; neither is there any difference between being and not being "in the light" (*ming*). Such is, I believe, the consequence of Lao Tzu's teaching of the nameless. The true sage is the one who knows that he is not a sage, or rather, the one who does not know that he is a sage. He has gone *beyond*.

Notes

1 "To know the constant is called enlightenment [*ming*]." This line appears twice, in Chs. 16 and 55.

2 The character *ming* is a compound pictogram, consisting of two pictograms, one representing the sun and the other the moon. Its basic sense is "brightness" as opposed to "darkness."

3 See Ch. 27.

4 See Chs. 10, 16, 27, 33, 36, 52, 55.

5 There is one passage in which the two terms, *chih* and *ming*, appear together. It reads: "He who knows others is wise [*chih*];/ He who knows himself is enlightened [*ming*]" (Ch. 33). Here, *chih* clearly means wisdom regarding human affairs, whereas *ming* refers to self-awareness, which is beyond "objective" (name-mediated) knowledge.

6 Ch. 36.

7 Ch. 52.

8 For the same reason, one may say that the infant's life too takes place in the dark. In this respect, the being of the infant is also different from that of the sage, even though Lao Tzu does compare the nameless life of the sage to that of the infant. See Chs. 10, 28.

9 In my view, human beings develop this capacity for consciousness or awareness, thanks to their use of language. It may be said that their development of consciousness is precisely what leads to their alienation from Tao or nature. Unlike the rest of humanity, however, the sage returns to nature with awareness. What he now sees *with awareness* is, of course, not the named, phenomenal world but the nameless, what transcends the phenomenal. It is this awareness of the nameless, the transcendental, that makes him different from both the "unknowing" creatures of nature and the "knowing" humanity.

10 See my comment on Ch. 37. To free one's mind of the body's desires is, to be sure, not to "extinguish" them altogether, as the Buddhist notion of nirvana seems to suggest. Note that we are here speaking of a certain state of consciousness, in which one is simply no longer *subject to* the influence of any bodily desires.

11 Notice the occurrence of the same verb "to see" (*kuan*) in the phrase "see the secret" (*kuan ch'i miao*) in Ch. 1 and in the phrase "I see" (*wo kuan*) in Ch. 16.

CHINESE TERMS

chih (wisdom
hsiao (filial piety)
hsüeh (learning)
i (one)
i (righteousness)
jen (humaneness)
li (ritual propriety)
ming (name)
ming (light)
p'u (uncarved block)
sheng jen (sage)
szu (self)
tao (way)
te (power; virtue)
t'ien (heaven)
t'ien ti (heaven and earth)
tzu-jan (nature)
tz'u (parental love; mercifulness)
wei (action)
wu (non-being)
wu szu (selflessness)
wu-wei (no-action)
wu yu (non-being)
wu yü (desirelessness)
yu (being)
yu-wei (action)
yü (desire)

BIBLIOGRAPHY

The *Analects (Lun-yü)*.

Baxter, William H. 1998. "Situating the Language of the Lao-tzu: The Probable Date of the *Tao-te-ching*," included in Kohn, Livia, and Michael LaFargue (eds.), *Lao-tzu and the Tao-te-ching*. Albany: State University of New York Press.

Chan, Wing-tsit. 1963a. *A Source Book in Chinese Philosophy*. Princeton: Princeton University Press.

_____, trans. 1963b. *The Way of Lao Tzu*. Indianapolis: The Bobbs-Merrill Co.

_____. 1979. "Introduction," *Commentary on the Lao Tzu by Wang Pi* (trans. Ariane Rump). Honolulu: The University Press of Hawaii.

The *Chuang Tzu*.

Fukunaga, Mitsuji. 1978. *Rōshi* (Lao Tzu). 2 Vols. Tokyo: Asahishinbunsha.

Graham, A. C. 1989. *Disputers of the Tao*. La Salle, Illinois: Open Court Publishing Co.

The *Great Learning (Ta Hsüeh)*.

The *Han Fei Tzu*.

Henricks, Robert G., trans. 2000. *Lao Tzu's Tao Te Ching*. New York: Columbia University Press.

_____, trans. 1989. *Lao-Tzu: Te-Tao Ching*. New York: Ballantine Books.

Katō, Jōken. 1966. *Rōshi Gengi no Kenkyū* (An Inquiry concerning the Original Meaning of the *Lao Tzu*). Tokyo: Meitokusha.

Kohn, Livia and Michael Lafargue, eds. 1998. *Lao-tzu and the Tao-te-ching*. Albany: State University of New York Press.

Lau, D. C., trans. 1963. *Lao Tzu: Tao Te Ching*. Harmondsworth,

England: Penguin Books.

The *Mencius.*

Morohashi, Tetsuji. 1973. *Rōshi no Kōgi* (Lecture on Lao Tzu). Tokyo: Taishukan-shoten.

Ssu-ma Ch'ien. *Shih Chi* (Records of the Historian).

Takeuchi Yoshio. 1927. *Rōshi no Kenkyū* (Studies in Lao Tzu). Tokyo: Kaizōsha.

Tōdō, Akiyasu. 1966. *Kanji no kigen* (The Origin of Chinese Characters). Tokyo: Tokuma-shoten.

Wang Pi. *Lao Tzu Tao Te Ching chu* (Commentary on Lao Tzu's *Tao Te Ching*).

Watson, Burton, trans. 1968. *The Complete Works of Chuang Tzu.* New York: Columbia University Press.

Waley, Arthur, trans. 1958. *The Way and Its Power: A Study of the Tao Te Ching and Its Place in Chinese Thought.* New York: Grove Press.

INDEX

All entries refer to the translation, not to the commentary.
Asterisks indicate terms that appear in the list of "Chinese Terms."
Numbers refer to chapters rather than pages.

Printed in the United States
59492LVS00002B/9

9 781401 083168